Brownsville Bred
Dreaming Out Loud

ELAINE DEL VALLE

DEDICATION

For *Papi*, in my constant effort to prove we exist!
For *Mami*, who read me *Cinderella* a million times and made me always know positivity and love.
For my siblings, Ana, Ben, Danny & Amanda—forever my home team.
For Brittany, I strive for you.
For Aunt Maggie and Uncle Jose for always being a shining example of hard work, family and pride.
For my husband, Al Eskanazy for inspiring and supporting me every day and in every way.

CONTENTS

ACKNOWLEDGMENTS

Special Thanks to
Al Eskanazy, Wynn Handman, Billy Lyons, Pamela Moller
Kareman, The Schoolhouse Theater, The Nuyorican Poets
Cafe, Danielle Gallant, Theater 808, Quinn Cassavale, Carey
Macaleer, Simon Maclean, 59E59 Theaters, Elysabeth
Kleinhans, Adriana Waterston, Lucinda Martinez, Jacklyn
Monk, Claudio Mueller, Taryn Kosviner, Jane Stine, Ana Leal.

1 OUT MY WINDOW

From out my window …

I could see the whole world …

and even though I am twelve stories up, I could hear the rap beats blasting from the shoulders of every other guy brave enough to take the shortcut through my *Langston Hughes* Brownsville projects.

You see, mine are the tallest buildings in all of East New York. The toughest, the hardest, the baddest.

On the ground, necks just about be breaking off trying to see who playing their favorite songs. But from up here, I see.

They find the beat easily and shake they booties, like I wish I could.

Everything moves just right on black bodies. They are lean and pretty and have muscles even though they ain't no gyms around here.

Black hair stays just in place, and they get real pretty, different color, beads on the ends of their braids. Those beads make a music of their own … by walking and especially when double dutching.

My hair is a straight flat mess, even after I spend some time with a curling iron and *Aqua Net*.

When I wish, I wish for caramel skin and curly hair. That I could find the beat and dance as good as the dancers on *Soul Train*—better even. Wouldn't nobody call me white cracker, even though they know I'm Puerto Rican. And wouldn't nobody make fun of me when I recite my rap songs.

I look over to the neighboring building and wonder if there is another girl out there, looking out of her 12F apartment with her bangs falling in her eyes, thinking the same thing that I'm thinking. Doing the same thing I'm doing. Wishing the same thing I'm wishing. Rapping to the beat she taps on her window sill.

Able to see the world through her window too.

2 NEXT CAR

Back when we was real little kids, me, my brothers and my sister and Mami and Papi used to play a game...just looking out our window. All we needed was the cars that drove by. Papi called our game "Next Car".

We start by choosing a color and wait for the next car of that color to pass by. Whatever car that is will be your car when you grow up. On Sundays you could wait for like an hour till all our colors finally drive by...Especially if the color is orange or something stupid like that. Whoever got the nicest car is the winner. Whoever picked the ugliest car, we all make fun of, and say that they will stay broke forever.

Once I called "black car," and it took almost a whole hour before a black car drove by. But when it did, it was a big black *limousine*—no dents or nothing, tinted windows, and real clean. You could see the sun shining on the top of the sunroof. That was my car and it meant that I would be rich.

"It musta lost its way" said my brother.

No other explanation for a car like that to be here. My brother said that the Heavyweight Champion of the whole world, *Iron Mike Tyson*, is from Brownsville, and that was prolly him come to check out the old neighborhood.

Last year they said he came by and that this dude from his old block knocked him out!

A corner dude knocking out the World Heavyweight

3

Champion?

I believe it, but it musta been a sucker punch.

Mami said, "you leave Brownsville long enough, you prolly forget to remember to watch out for what's coming".

It was a real, real, real, real nice day. A day you could breathe, y'know. The sun shining, and the air crisp. A day when Mami opens up all the windows, so her laundry could dry as it hung on the line tied to the steam pipes of each room.

Mami made us all scrambled eggs for breakfast. Papi cut open a big Italian bread and smeared *Parkay* on top. When he toasts it in the oven, the whole apartment smell so good, like *Downy* clean from the clothes, fresh air from the outside and baked bread and butter from the oven.

That morning I called "next blue car," my sister Ana called "third red," my brother Danny called "next brown." I 'on't know why anybody would want a brown car. Mami called "black" and Papi called "second blue." Big Head (aka my brother Benjamin 'cause he kinda mean and got a big head) picked "next white car." We ate Papi's bread and hung out our kitchen's windows waiting. Looking up in the distance I could see a white airplane. But airplanes don't count. At night Mami be thinking they UFOs gonna come and get her for experiments. One night she woke up and said they had taken her for sure. But she musta been dreaming. Like out of all the people in the whole world, they gonna choose my moms to experiment on.

"White." Ben's white car was a big white *Mack* truck come rolling down the block. We was all laughing at the thought of Ben blasting music from out a big white truck. Papi joked how Ben could trick it out by painting the Puerto Rican flag on the hood—like the one we painted on our living room wall earlier that year…The WHOLE living room wall.

On nice days, like this one, even that embarrassing wall don't bother me none. It's a day when you can't help but notice all the colors in the world … Like a picture so beautiful that it makes you wanna cry.

We was all laughing 'bout Ben's truck when—when this little girl, black as tar and skinny as a crack head caught my eye.

Running fast as a rock shot out of a slingshot, straight outta the building next door. On her way to get that free lunch prolly. We stopped going for the free lunches years ago, 'cause it's embarrassing to be standing round waiting to get free food. Only little kids go for that—cause little kids is too stupid to feel shame.

The free cheese line—that's a whole other story. That line be round the block. Even grown-ups be on that line. Especially crackheads and winos, 'cause they know they could sell it to corner stores that make sandwiches with it.

That little dark skinned girl, she running just at the same speed as Ben's white *Mack* truck is rolling down the block. Look like they was about to intersect. I was just about to scream out,

"Watch out!"

When it happened.

I heard the PING! of her body jump off the bumper of Ben's white *Mack* truck.

The last time she moved was the first time I ever seen't somebody die.

Crazy how I could see it all coming from up here.

She was like eight years old or something. She ain't even stop to look see if there was a car coming, or if the light was red or nothing. She ain't never stop to realize that she was about to be toe-up underneath that white *Mack* truck. Ben's truck wasn't even going fast enough to make it screech when it stopped or nothing. After it hit her, and the driver changed his gear to park, I could hear its engine running. That's all I could hear. We all saw it, but couldn't none of us make a sound.

I gasped as the driver got out. He was shaking like a leaf, and it wasn't 'cause he was a white man in Brownsville, neither. I remember thinking exactly what Mami said right before she said it, "*Ay dios mio*, he better get back into his truck and lock his doors until the police come." It ain't take too long for him to figure that out for his self.

The crowd started up. People started screaming and coming at the truck. Banging on his bumpers. This woman ran out of the neighboring building with her knees bent, one of her hands over her mouth and the other one over her heart. Body bouncing like she never missed a meal—musta been the girl's grandmother or maybe her mother. Not that I couldn't make out her age, she was like 35 or something. But round here we got grandmothers and moms that be 'bout the same age.

The lady with the bent knees took her hand away from her mouth and start screaming. Her cry echoed between the buildings. In no time, all the building windows on Sutter Avenue was opened, and people huddled out of them, staring. Nothing to do but watch. They was all prolly wondering what happened. Prolly blaming the driver—but I seen't the whole thing. My whole family, together, seen't the whole thing. I think I seen it even before it happened. I shoulda said it. I shoulda yelled, "Watch out!"

The crowd grew madder, and Papi scream't out,

"IT WASN'T HIS FAULT!"

But couldn't nobody listen to nothing but that (grand)mama's heart breaking. Why was that little girl alone? Mami woulda never let me go nowhere alone when I was that little. She still watch me and my sister from out the window for as long as she can.

"I hope somebody call the police" said Mami. We ain't had no phone, or for sure Mami woulda.

"Maybe that truck driver got a walkie-talkie radio in his truck," Ben said.

That girl was going high speed like the *Road Runner*, but everything else about that day was creeping and just kept getting slower. Like everybody was stuck in quicksand. Like her being dead was part of a recipe that made everything else thick. People looking out they windows watched like blinking wasn't allowed. Others was scratching they heads outside of they buildings … afraid to get closer. Just waiting for the police to come … waiting … waiting … for nothing to change.

The police came, sure enough. They put a bright yellow plastic cover over her little body. The sky was so blue, and the clouds so white—even the street looked fresh-paved black.

The breeze was just enough to cool you down without noticing it—until the police put that yellow plastic over her body. That's when we all noticed the breeze. The invisible wind was like an evil ghost that kept lifting up that bright yellow blanket and reminding us that a little girl wasn't never gonna grow up. I used to pray for cool breezes on hot summer days. But these came with screams like the ones you hear in scary movies—when the characters know a axe is coming and it's gonna hurt. That blanket came up with that breeze, and felt like a axe every time. I didn't want to look, but I couldn't stop looking. None of us could. I could see her white *Tippy* socks, folded down lace, on her long bony ebony legs. And like the hand of one of those music conductors...whenever the blanket rose, so did the sound of that (grand)mama's screams. Her voice rang straight up, but her knees never straightened.

That was the last time we played *Next Car*.

3 PAPI'S SWAGGER

He got swagger. That's what I hear some people say about my father—like he walk around knowing he good at everything that he does. You ever meet somebody like that?

The thing is that he IS good at everything he does.

People round here wish they had swagger. They think … and I hope that they is right … that wit' enough trying hard you can get some swagger.

Most every dude be walking with a limp—even the ones that ain't never been shot. But my father's walk ain't like that at all. It's more like…like he always walking to the center of some dance floor, like *John Travolta* in *Saturday Night Fever*. Like wherever he be seem like the glow of a disco ball is shining little light squares all around him, make you wanna run up to him, carry him and cheer, like he just pitched a no-hitter at the *World Series* or something.

Papi makes his paycheck by working six days a week at Public School 125 on Rockaway Avenue. He brings his swagger wit' him along wit' his radio to play his salsa music all day long. The hundred keys on his belt loop open every classroom in the school. They rattle like a tambourine, as he dances his mop around, cleaning hall floors.

I ain't been to P.S. 125 with Papi for a while now, but when we was littler me and my brothers and sister would go to work with him on Saturday and get to play anywhere we wanted until he was done cleaning. Freshly waxed floors act like a skating rink and our socks were the ice skates Papi could never afford.

When Papi done with his work, I would hear him from the principal's loudspeaker. His heavy and happy Spanish accent dreamin' out loud, saying things like—"And now welcome onto the pitching mound for the *New Jork Jankees*, Daniel Medina!"

My brother Danny stop anything that he doing to live in Papi's dream for him.

My brothers' and my sister's last name is Medina, 'cause even though Benjamin and Danny and Ana call Papi Papi. I am Papi's only real child. When I think about that I feel like I am some kind of special.

Mami say that my grandmother named my papi right. His name is Angel. If he got one candy left in his pocket, he would give it away to somebody who want it.

When Mami makes pork chops, we all get one, but Mami saves two for Papi. When he get home from work, I stay at the table while he eat, and he always give me his second one 'cause he know that fried pork chops is my all time favorite—and that's how much he love me.

One time this real old lady who be selling *limber de coco* (coconut icee) on Belmont Avenue stopped me and my mother on the street to say, *"Tiene que ser la hija de Angel Del Valle,"* which mean, "You must be the daughter of Angel Del Valle." Like there was only one Angel Del Valle in the whole world.

I say, "Yeah, I'm his daughter," and she say it again, "you MUST be," and then she say 'cause we got *"una cara"* ... and that means "one face."

And that's the nicest thing anybody ever said about me.

My father is like a star in Brownsville, 'specially to everybody who play baseball at *Betsy Head Park*—on account of he used to play for the minor leagues in Puerto Rico. He a righty, but he could pitch left-handed too, and he could bat both ways, which my brother Ben says is like a miracle that he could never forget seeing.

Papi might spend a whole bunch of time wit' my brothers trying to rub off all of his baseball magic on them, but they is Medinas and not Del Valles and they not never gonna have "one face" with Papi like me ... and that is the special thing about me.

That old lady selling them *limber de cocos* be watching my papi in all his baseball glory during the daytime and at night she gets to watch him for what he is really famous for, his outdoor music jams—rumbas.

See my father is a musician too. He got mad skills on every instrument he touch. He could play the piano and the guitar and the flute and the congas and everything.

I been watching my papi make his music my whole life. He even make his own conga drum skins.

At our kitchen table, Papi sits clamping and tightening and shaping his conga skins.

I not trying to learn nothing but I just like to watch him under the aluminum gooseneck lamp in our yellow kitchen, under the picture painting of Jesus Christ that Mami was so happy to win at the *Prospect Park* gambling and flea market.

Ever since I sat in the backseat of the car all the way home with that painting, every time I look at it, I could swear that if my father was blonde and had a beard, they'd look just alike too. Papi look like the Latino version of Jesus Christ. And Jesus looking up at his father, the way I am looking up at mine all the time ... and they are both our Gods.

When Papi's conga skins is just right, he gets dressed for his big rumba music jam.

He wear his favorite red polyester pants ... them pants scream STOP, WATCH ME NOW. They so tight Mami laughs that she hardly even gotta iron them. The shirt he wear got arrows on the shoulders like he a captain on a ship, or a cowboy or something. And his shoes—nothing like the work boots he wear at the school. They is soft soled with mesh netting on top, lets his feet breathe as they tap and glide across the gum-stained concrete.

Papi puts on his white aviator sunglasses, even though the sun is going down and they ain't even got no prescription in them—not like Mami's coke-bottle glasses.

He replaces his every day *Yankees* baseball cap with his once a week rumba soft fedora hat, cool like that ... like he know he about to rock the planet before he even gets started.

Ain't a far walk to where he plays his music, but it would be hard to carry both congas and his *timbales* there, and so he loads them up in his white *Chevy Laguna*.

When we pull up, he swaggers over to his trunk, and pulls out his congas. It feels like *Tyson* is making his way to another thirty-second knockout—except better 'cause all the excitement is there and you know it's gonna last all night.

I could see the women, some as old as that old lady scraping *limber de cocos*. She one of them. The rest is all hanging out they windows ... waiting, watching. They jump inside like they been waiting for my papi to get there all day, all week, all they life.

I could picture them inside they apartments, running to they vanity, to paint they lips bright red, and then running down they stairs. They stand next to me, huffing out *Cafe Bustelo* and sweating through their *Tigress* perfume.

Last month I got *Tigress* perfume for my tenth birthday. It come with a matching powder. I put two dabs on my neck on very special days, when I want to feel special—two dabs only on account of I want it to last forever. I wear it to them rumbas too.

Them ladies stand beside me be busy kissing off all of their lipstick on one another cheeks. They kiss hi until the only lipstick left is on they teeth—smiling wide as can be. They look at my father and wait for his music to start.

When I catch somebody looking at me, I think that—what the old *limber de coco* lady said—that I must be his daughter, 'cause I got his face...I mean I 'on't see the resemblance myself. Even when I put the ends of my long thin hair above my lips to make a mustache like Papi's. But it don't matter me none 'cause I know it gotta be true. Too many people be saying it for it to be a lie.

It's as true as french fries, blue eyes and ice cream ... things we can all agree are the best things in the world.

12

We all stand there waiting ...

All the Puerto Ricans in Brownsville ...

Which even in a crowd ain't hardly many of us Puerto Ricans in Brownsville ... but it's everybody we got, giving it all we got, till our twenty or thirty strong feel like a thousand.

Then finally, my father grabs his *claves*. *Claves* are two metal sticks, no bigger than a soda bottle and don't look like much, but when you clap them together you would swear their sound is vibrating inside of you. They's louder than gunshots from a .38 but not jarring at all. Papi holds them *claves* up over his head and counts down "*Uno, dos, tres.*"

The trumpets sound and the guitars strum, and they all just following the beat that comes from my father's soft slaps sliding from one of his conga skins to the other.

Then Papi's voice rises above all them instruments, and it is surely the sweetest sound of them all.

He sings a song that makes everybody, the whole crowd, move. We all moving and feeling good in just the same kinda way.

I sway—even though I surely ain't a good dancer at all.

Few people got swagger but lotsa people got rhythm, but I just don't got none of them. Much as Papi used to put me on his toes tryin' to teach me how to follow a beat, is as much as it ain't work. So much so that I can't hear a beat, without feeling like I am still on his toes.

Seem a shame that the only child of this salsa swagger, great baseball playing legend, can't hardly dance or do no sports at all. But that don't stop me from trying and knowing that I must got something special in me on account of his DNA is flowing in my veins.

The mostly black people that live in Brownsville be staring at Papi's conga drums and wonder what he singing about.

Black people run these projects, and beatboxing and rap is the rhythm of our Brownsville streets—it's even what I like. I mean, for the most part, I can't stand my father's records, especially after the million times I gotta hear them playing in our apartment—but there's something about these rumbas that makes us handful of Rodriguezes, Gomezes, Torreses, and

Martinezes get mad respect while our music plays.

Rumbas are the easiest time to be a Puerto Rican in Brownsville.

Me and my brothers and sister walk home with Mami before the rumba is over 'cause "ain't no good woman ever keep her kids out all night" and we all know that it's surely no good for any kind of woman to walk alone after dark, even if she is dragging her four kids beside her.

It only takes one block of walking before I can't hear the salsa no more. Rap music just kinda takes over. Like one boombox battles over the sounds of another, before they are all drowned out by every passing car that got tinted windows. We walk across the street and the driver blows a kiss at my mother—Gross!

I could see his gold teeth shining, as we cross. I watch his nasty lips as they form the words that all Puerto Rican women hate to hear, but gotta hear all the time, "*Mira, mira.*"

Impressed with hisself, like he saying something my mother ain't never heard.

Don't matter him none that me and my sister is staring him down, like our evil eyes could make his car crash. Mami and my brothers pretend not to hear.

When we get home, Mami lets us each have a *Flavor-Ice*. I always choose blue, and my lips be blue even after I brush my teeth to go to sleep.

Ana is already asleep in our bed. I lay next to her trying to stay up, to wait for my father. But I could smell her sleep on my pillow and feel it coming over me as I think about my father making people dance all night and feel better about life.

4 NEEDLE ON RECORD

It is morning.

I am late for school.

Got just enough time for a dry cup of *Frosted Flakes*, before I jump into the clothes I wore this weekend.

Even though I don't got a lot of clothes, I would never want anybody in my class to say that I am dirty. And so I would never usually wear the same clothes three days in a row, but I ain't never seen nobody from my school on the weekend, on account of except for them rumbas, we mostly stay inside our apartment.

The people in my class ain't prolly never even heard of a rumba, and so they surely not gonna know what I wore to one the night before.

I go to school, where everything is easy and nothing is expected.

Me and my whole class stay in the same classroom all day except when it's time for Art with Miss Bramson, and Lunch in the lunchroom.

School lunch is nasty, and we all sit in the same order that we line up in. I been sitting and standing next to Mimi Marshall since kindergarten.

She tall like me, but black and beautiful. We used to be best friends 'cause we was always next to each other, but the older she got the less she like to talk and so she made friends with Lana Johnston who is the shortest in the whole class and at the opposite end of our line-up.

Mimi Marshall is the best dresser in the whole school. She match from her socks to the beads in her hair. Me and her is always the last two standing at the spelling bees, and she always wins. She spell fast like she don't have to think, while I try to take all the time they give me to make sure what about to come out of my mouth is right. I got psychiatrist and she got castle. I got ventriloquist and she got parakeet. But it all came down to cholesterol and so Mimi Marshall gets to go to the district spelling bee at the end of this year again.

No matter what happens there, her mother, Mrs. Marshall, will surely bring a bucket of homemade fried chicken for everybody to share ... and the entire class will have Mimi Marshall to thank.

I think if I ever made it to the district spelling bee, I might ask Mami to bring up her red rice and beans and I think everybody will like it ... even though I don't.

Mami say I'm a weird bird on account of I am the only Puerto Rican she ever met that don't like red rice and beans.

I hate when food touches and even if I manage to take out the beans, you can't get the red off that rice after it has been cooked together. And that's one of the hardest things about being Puerto Rican.

And Mami would make sure that nobody call her Mrs. Del Valle—and not on account of that ain't really her name, 'cause she and Papi ain't really married—but on account of Mami would want everybody to call her Carmen ... 'cause that's just how Mami is.

I am always the first one home from school. My mother is at her usual spot around three o'clock—at the stovetop stirring rice and beans, watching *Channel 7's General Hospital.*

I start my homework at the kitchen table. Neat as can be. I got the best handwriting in the school and prolly the whole world. I got the neatest notebook too. I rather start all over on a fresh sheet of paper than to see a bunch of eraser marks making my paper look ugly. My sister Ana always say that I am messy, and I know I am in my room and in my dresser drawers. I stuff everything in, and I don't care. All her clothes is all hung up and neat and mines stay in the closet where Mami keeps all the dry laundry before they are ironed. Mami say we need to be responsible for ironing our own clothes, which is why I like stretch pants—you ain't gotta be responsible for stretch jeans.

From anywhere in our apartment, I could hear Papi's keys jingling to unlock the locks on our apartment door.

I used to run to the door when Papi got home from work to help him unlace his work boots, and even though I am too old for that now, I still feel happy inside when I hear his keys.

And even though I know I am about to hate his salsa records playing for the rest of our day, I still feel happy inside.

And my mouth waters knowing that Papi has a bag full of his and my favorite candies coming my way. *Mary Janes, Juicy Fruit, Chico Sticks, Whoppers, Fun Dip*, watermelon, banana and grape *Now and Laters*.

At our living room, the Puerto Rican flag that we all painted still waves flat on the whole wall. Embarrassing. On the other wall used to be a upright piano, where Papi taught my sister Ana how to play. Earlier this year Papi sold it, just before my fingers grew long enough to try it.

Milk crates is stacked atop each other, looking like a bookcase that never held books. Instead they is filled with Papi's salsa records—all in alphabetical order. He keep his records like I keep my notebook.

"*Elaine, ve a tu cuarto, que nosotros tenemos que hablar,*" my mother says from behind me telling me, which mean "go to my room on account of she want to talk to my father".

From behind Mami's glasses, her eyes look like they been crying...and not from anything that happened to Luke and Laura on *General Hospital* 'cause she has turned the thirteen inch TV that sits on our kitchen table off. I ain't never seen that TV off at this time unless the president was talking or something and so I instantly feel that something is wrong... who died?

I surely must'a missed something somewhere between last

night's rumba and this morning's *Frosted Flakes*.

Mami and Papi...they just waiting on me to leave.

Through the narrow hallway and into my room. I leave my door open, but I can't hear nothing...so I give up trying and play my records.

"*You Light Up My Life*" by *Debbie Boone* is my favorite song of all time.

My gray box record player say "Board of Education" in big white letters, so you can't miss it. Its needle broke a couple years back, and my father taught me how to make a needle from a staple and secure it with a rubber band. I am so happy to have my record player. For the most part I use it to drown out my father's salsa in the living room, but I just like to hear my records and sing. Sing at my mirror. I hold my hairbrush and sing like I am at a show. I could sing all day. And I think that I am pretty good at singing and hope that one day my voice might have the same special that my father's got.

I hardly got started when I see my father's reflection in the mirror. I shut up fast. "Oh, hey Papi."

"You sound so good," he say.

But I know that Papi would say that no matter what I sound like.

Papi sat down on my sister's side of the bed, and I shut off my record player.

He been getting skinny lately and his skinny make him look even taller sitting on our platform bed.

My father taught me a lot of things, but he always say that I taught him English. But I guess we could say that we learned it at the same time.

In any language, he don't never have no trouble expressing hisself. Papi is a man that could cry, laugh, dance and sing without no shame.

He would never stop singing if somebody was watching. It would make him want to sing more and louder. When people tell him that he sing good, he don't never gotta wonder if they just saying it to be nice.

"You gotta listen to your Mami in everything that she says, because your Mami is always right...and you gotta always go to school," he says.

All I could say is "I know" because I do.

I don't know why, but my skin starts crawling like the time I noticed lice on Dora Smithe's head while sitting in back of her in the school auditorium. Just as I started wondering who died, he say, "I am moving to Puerto Rico to live *con tu abuelita*."

There must be something wrong with my grandmother in Puerto Rico. Papi is her youngest son and she is very old. Her wrinkled hands are permanently bent from arthritis. She came to visit us two times in my life and even though she loves me and I love her, it hurts when I look at her.

"Because she need help," I say.

"Because I need help," he say.

Much as he must want me to listen is as much as I don't want to hear no more.

"Because I made mistakes, because I made mistakes with *drogas*. You understand? You can never make these same mistakes, because they can tear your life apart."

Drogas—which mean DRUGS. DRUGS! I could hear my ears swelling up inside when he say this to me.

I been watching people get on drugs forever. Good people that I used to see waiting for the church van one day... and then having sex in the back staircase for a five-dollar crack vial the next. Like a switch that can't be turned off.

They sell anything they got to get the drugs they need... even the things they like the most ... prolly like they pianos.

They start getting high with friends for fun at parties and outside hanging out ... like at rumbas.

They get real skinny, losing they appetite for even they favorite foods ... like pork chops.

And they lose they teeth, sucking on penny candies ... like watermelon *Now and Laters*, on account of the drugs that they is taking be giving them a sweet tooth.

I can't stop thinking long enough to listen. I don't take my time like I do in the spelling bees. I let out the first thing that come to my mouth. The hate that can protect me.

"I can't stand your salsa records anyway! You need to take them all wit' you."

I race to my record player, wishing it wasn't something he gave me. I look down at *Debbie Boone's "You Light Up My Life"* and smother it with another record, *Run-DMC's "Sucker MC"*. I play it loud as the one speaker that still worked would allow … until it—I—made my father leave. Leave my sight. Leave my room, leave our apartment, leave my life.

That old lady selling *limber de coco* on Belmont avenue—her wrinkled sunburn hands gripping her spoon to serve the coconut ice, looking up like she was shocked by my face. Like she seen a ghost. "You MUST BE the daughter of Angel?"

One face.

One face that I used to feel proud to have.

One face that I wish I never had to look at again.

One face that's embarrassing and stupid, like that Puerto Rican flag painted on our living room wall.

All them commercials with a egg sizzling in a frying pan talking 'bout how a brain is when it be on drugs is stupid. "This is your brain on drugs." They should surely show the truth—like girls in the back staircase having sex for crack, their babies born cracked out, not even knowing who the father is, and fathers having to leave they kids.

I want to ask my father, "Can't you beat it?"

But round here all them questions ain't nothing, on account of people on drugs is liars mostly. On account of the answer is usually no.

I heard my brothers come home and go to their room and when my sister got home, she came into our room like she already knew … for a while. She had a newspaper "Help Wanted" section.

She fourteen now and even though she don't hardly talk to me anymore except to complain how messy I am, she say three things to me. Like she was saying them to herself. "I'm going to get a job and I'm going to make my own money and I am going to get a phone."

Then she said one more thing that actually was meant for me. "And you not going to be allowed to use it."

I feel bad that my father come into her life and he not her

father and she gotta feel the shame that I feel on account of him.

She might not got his face, but he still been her papi since she was three years old. My brothers' papi since they was two and one, and my papi for my whole life.

I ain't try to stay up all night, but I couldn't help it. I lay next to my sister on our bed. I think about the mattress under us, and remember when my aunt Nellie gave us this old full-size platform bed of hers. I was so happy 'cause I used to be so scared in my twin size bed. I'd lay in bed at night with my eyes open waiting for something to come out of our closet … But ever since we had this bed, whenever I am scared I just let my foot touch my sisters foot so I know that she is still there. So I know that I am safe.

The next morning, on my way to school, I rushed past my father's eyes for what I surely knew would be the last time. He sat on the red velvet couch underneath his Puerto Rican flag wall.

When I got home from school Mami's tears was watering down the can of beige paint she was using to roll over Papi's Puerto Rican flag.

It had taken Papi four days to paint that flag on our wall. A full day of taping so the lines would be straight enough, three coats of blue, and two cans of red—on account of the first red just wasn't bright enough.

When Papi was done he blasted a *Tito Puente* salsa song so loud that you could hardly hear Papi's conga when he started to play along with it. When the song was over he made us sing *"Qué Bonita Bandera"*—a song previously reserved only for the Puerto Rican Day Parade.

Qué bonita bandera
Qué bonita bandera
Qué bonita bandera
La bandera de Puerto Rico.

It took Papi four days to paint that wall…but once I picked up the paint brush beside Mami to help her, we covered it in less than an hour—and just in time to spare my sister and two brothers the pain of watching it fade away.

5 ABUELA

From the back seat of my grandmother's blue *Toyota*, I watch the clouds follow me. My mami looks back at me from the passenger seat while my grandmother drives. I think, ain't nobody ever seen an *abuela* (grandmother) look better than mine. My mom's mom...she young as far as grandmothers go. She forty-five, and she make her hair blonde and wavy, and she puff on *Newports* all fancy-like, out her driver's seat window. I watch her from the backseat through the haze of smoke she got coming my way. Her window rolled down, and I wonder how somebody who look so good could be such a stone cold hater.

I got twenty-five cousins, thass twenty-five other grandbabies she got, and out of all of us, I'm pretty sure that she (my grandmother) hates me the most. Worst thing about that is that all my cousins live like in Queens, Philadelphia, Canarsie, and Georgetown, but I got to live right in the same building as her. So she get to hate me everyday and many times a day. I swear I could feel her hating me through the building walls ... rising up to suffocate me in my sleep.

My grandmother live six floors down in apartment 6F, with her husband Goyo and my aunt Elizabeth. Elizabeth is slow so even though she older than my mami she kinda like my age in her head. Mami say Elizabeth is a miracle on account of she

23

wasn't supposed to live past the age of three. Elizabeth was born with lung disease and so she got over a hundred stitches all over her back from where she got her lung replacement.

Mami likes to visit my grandma's apartment, but I ain't got no idea why. She visit a lot more since Papi been gone. Maybe because *Abuela* got a car and she drives us to a big *Pathmark* supermarket in Canarsie once a month where Mami can do a big *compra* (grocery) and my brothers get to make extra money by helping white people to their cars with their bags.

It's only six floors down on the elevator to visit *Abuela*—I dread the trip. Going down on the elevator, I watch the light pass through from the hallways of each floor. Down, down, down—that's where we have to go and that's what I feel every time I gotta see her.

I once seen't this old movie where this baseball player wanted to be real good at baseball and so this guy who was the devil had made a deal with him. I swear it feel like Mami making that same kinda deal with my grandmama, but her deal is the car and our ability to get away.

Today we going to see my favorite cousin in Philadelphia. Out of all of them twenty-five cousins, Cynthia is my favorite. She so special even *Abuela* likes her. She's on my grandmother's top three list. The rest of us is way down on the bottom of that list. Bottom of her list is like the bottom of her shoes.

I got a baby cousin named Lea. We call her Baby Lea. My grandmother hates Baby Lea almost as much as she hates me —Lea's father is Dominican, and so grandma calls Baby Lea "*La Dominicana*". I once heard her say that all Dominicans got big pork chop fat lips. Everybody know when she say "*La Dominicana*", she saying it with hate.

My aunt Maggie married an Ecuadorian man and so I got a cousin named Diana, she a baby too, but we don't call her baby Diana, just Diana. Grandma calls her "*La Ecuadoriana*". I don't know what exactly she means when she calls her that, but I could tell it's just as bad as "*La Dominicana*". Thank God she can't call me "*La Puerto Riqueña*" 'cause that just make me just like her—which actually would be the worst thing she could ever make me out to be.

We pull up to the gas station, and she uses the little bit of English that she know to say, "Fill it up."

She puffs her *Newport* harder and turns up the volume on the radio of her AM dial playing nothing except some old Spanish man talking ... 'cause I ain't suffering enough!

I watch the thick gold chain around her neck, Jesus dangling on his cross, and wonder at God, "God, why my grandmother hate me?" and "why she—who gets her chain snatched all the time—always replace it with a more expensive one? ... even though she on welfare just like us?"

Don't nobody get their chain snatched more than my grandmother. Less in the wintertime, but at least once a month in the summer. She come back from Pitkin Avenue all red necked saying that she ain't really hurt on account of the Lord was there around her neck protecting her. Mami told her to get a rosary, and I be wanting to add that she stupid but I don't, 'cause Mami say that I ain't allowed to disrespect my elders.

My grandmother would definitely be getting her purse snatched too, except that she ain't got one. She carry a little change purse but that change purse is really a decoy, because she take her real money out from her bra.

The "ding" of the gas pump says fourteen gallons for fourteen dollars. Even though we still on our block, it feels like a hour that we been trying to start this long drive to Philadelphia. *Abuela* dives into her bra to pay the man at the pump. She gives him a ten from her bra and four ones out her change purse, and he leans to look down her shirt as she counts it. She know what he doing, and I'm sure she don't mind. *Abuela* takes the last puff of her cigarette and throws it out her window.

It's a three and a half hour drive to Philly where my cousin Cynthia, her sister and brother, Sonia and Macho, and her mother who is my aunt Milta live.

Macho real name is Genero—name't after his father—but they ain't never called him that 'cause his father ain't around no more either.

Macho got the *Muscular Dystrophy* so he can't walk too good. He be in a wheelchair most of the time, but he could walk if he hold on to things. Mami always be trying to help him walk on his own, and he could take a few steps … almost like a little baby learning to walk. I seen't him take a few staggering steps, focusing real hard on each one.

Abuela say he look more like his drunk father when he try to walk, so Macho rather stay in his wheelchair most of the time when she around. She also say that Macho's mole—on the side of his mouth—look like somebody put a cigarette out on his face.

Abuela don't say too much about my cousin Sonia, which is a good thing if you ask me. But she don't never stop talking about my cousin Cynthia. She is her favorite. "Cynthia is so pretty. Cynthia is so smart. Cynthia is so happy." Cynthia-Cynthia-Cynthia.

You would think that all that Cynthia talk would make me sick of Cynthia but Cynthia is my favorite too. Cynthia makes being stuck in a car with my grandmother all the way to Philadelphia worth it.

Me and Cynthia like all the same music and all the same TV shows. We is just alike. We got the same color hair and the same color skin and the same color freckles. Some people can't even tell us apart—Except she the only one of us that gets hugs from our grandmama.

Cynthia and me even almost have the same birthday. I'm born July 13. She born July 14. Every July my grandmother take me to *Toys"R"Us* so I could help her pick out a gift for Cynthia. She don't never get me one, but Cynthia always lets me play with her gift.

Cynthia older than me by two years, she thirteen. We even the same height now. I used to be shorter, but last summer I got taller.

Cynthia comes to stay over Grandma's house for two weeks every summer. My grandmother drives all the way to Philadelphia to pick her up. (She won't even ride the elevator six floors up to our apartment to visit with us.) Cynthia come to spend time with me, but Grandma don't never give her permission to stay over my house. She say Cynthia is better off with her and Elizabeth. Nasty old witch!

Cynthia be so bored at *Abuela's* house. She just sit with Aunt Elizabeth all day watching game show after game show on account of Elizabeth is obsessed with them.

I bring my *Barbie* dolls down to play with Cynthia and we listen to music together. When Cynthia around and Grandma gotta go somewhere I beg so I could go too. Cynthia begs too, so Grandma usually say yes. Me and Cynthia run to the car to see who gets to sit in the front seat. I have asthma, and I'm just slow. They used to call me slow poke, and I never win so I always get stuck in the backseat, carsick like I am today.

Cynthia usually wins and she reclines the front seat and lays down. Last year my legs grew long, like my father's, and I finally beat Cynthia to the front seat. When I went to recline the seat, my grandmother screamed at me and said that I should know that Cynthia likes to lay down in the car, and that if I reclined the front seat, she wouldn't be able to. She calls me "*malegradecida*" which means I ain't been raised right. So, I rode with my long legs, knees to my chest, so Cynthia could be comfortable lying on the back seat. My grandmother is a total bitch. Mami says it's because she liked Cynthia's father better than mine. I be wanting to say—you mean the guy that Macho look like when he walking funny—but I don't say it. Instead, I just look out the car window and remind myself to respect my elders.

We drive past the junkyard under the overpass and I watch the neighborhood change. Rockaway Avenue becomes Rockaway Parkway and the stores look better, and the people get lighter, and I'm gearing up to smell the *McDonald's* french fries even over *Abuela's Newports* and Aunt Elizabeth's terrible breath.

Elizabeth's smelly breath ain't her fault. Something 'bout the way she was born that make her teeth all gray and her mind forget to brush them.

There it is—*McDonald's*. I breathe in deep, knowing that once we get to the *New Jersey Turnpike*, Grandma will need more gas or to pee. And I know them rest areas, off the highway, got lots of *McDonald's*. She would really have to try to be hating on me to avoid one. Mami looks back at me and knows what I am thinking. We both is thinking the same thing … that saying it out loud will doom our chances of *McDonald's* later.

My grandmother had eleven kids, like she was trying to break a world record. Out of all eleven of them, my mami is the best one. They all kinda great in they own way, even Elizabeth … can't nobody memorize a *TV Guide* better than Elizabeth. But none is more greater than Mami. She nice to everybody and she give real good advice, even when people ain't asking.

When my brothers' baseball games is over, sometimes some of they teammates' moms are not home, and so they be outside waiting and sometimes crying. My mami always let them chill out in our apartment and try to make them feel better. She make big tubs of delicious white rice with red beans on the side, 'cause she know I hate red rice and beans when they mixed together. She feed them and since they is black, my mami's cooking is as special to them as *McDonald's* is to me. Then she talk to them as they look out our kitchen window, watching for they moms.

My mami got hospitality written all over her. I wonder how my mami got so nice with a mother like my grandmother and a father like my grandfather. I don't know my grandfather—but on holidays, when my mom sees all her siblings I get to hear all about how bad he used to beat them all.

On New Year's, all my aunts and my uncles come to my grandmother's house. Nellie, Maggie, Milta, Miriam, Evelyn, Elizabeth, Big Luzzy, Little Luzzy, Nelson and Michael and they all act like kids again. We play *Bingo* using pennies 'cause ain't enough red dots for all of us.

We all trying to stay awake to watch *Dick Clark* bring the ball down on *Times Square*. Mami and my aunts and my uncles be telling stories about when they papi used to beat them. They be cracking up laughing, making fun of how he beat Mami until her mouth was broke, and how Nellie and Big Luzzy was on the ledge of a roof threatening him that they was gonna jump if he beat them again.

"What happened?"

Michael say that my real grandfather had begged them to come back off the roof and then he beat them some more anyway. They all be laughing so hard that they cry and all my aunts' mascara be running down they cheeks. My *titi* Little Luzzy can't hardly catch her breath from laughing, she always the first to pull out her asthma inhaler. By the end of the night they be passing around that asthma inhaler like it's a basketball and they are all the *Harlem Globetrotters*.

My grandmother don't be saying nothing, but she don't be laughing neither. She kinda just got a grimace on her face like *Charlie Brown*. She puff on her cigarette. When they all finish the story, my *titi* (aunt) Maggie says, "You shoulda jumped the way Mami did."

Then they all tell the story about how my grandmother actually threw herself out the window.

"Better than to get beat," say uncle Nelson.

Milta adds, "She was saved by the bars on the window holding her up by her bra straps."

"Somebody called 911," say Big Luzzy.

"When the police came we ain't wanna say nothing," Aunt Miriam laughed.

Then they all start laughing through another story 'bout how my grandpa kicked my grandmother down the stairs when she was six months pregnant with Miriam, which is how my aunt Miriam turn't out cross eyed and mentally slow. Other than that one eye that keep crossing when she thinking, Miriam look just 'bout normal.

My uncle Nelson's girlfriend, Maria—new to all this—was looking at them like they was all crazy. She from Colombia, so she real proper like. Her Spanish sound like English coming out of *Olivia Newton John*, and in real nice Spanish she ask, "When did she finally leave him?" and then the story continues.

"One day they were riding in the car and up walks this lady and stops right in front of the car," *Titi* Maggie says. "The woman pounds her fist on the hood and starts screaming, '*Quién es esa mujer?* (Who's that woman?)'"

My grandmother say, "*Soy la esposa del y la madre de sis hijos.*

29

(I'm his wife and the mother of his kids.)"

Then my grandmother got out the car and say, "You could have him."

And she walked away. Thass when she moved to Brownsville, figuring that my grandpapa was not tough enough to come in these parts … and she was right. He left her and all their kids alone after that.

My grandmama don't say nothin'. She just sits and puffs on her cigarette.

My *abuela* had put up with all that beating on her and on her kids, but she wasn't never gonna be hearing about no other woman "*la cabrona corteja*." I gotta give her that — that and she look good, and she know how to drive, and she take care of Elizabeth real good and know that she gonna have to do that for the rest of her life no matter how old Elizabeth get — but that's all I'll ever give her.

6 THE POOL

There is a lot of things about people that I can't understand. How Papi could throw us away on account of drugs. How my grandma could be so mean to a little kid and how Mami ain't never want to learn to drive. She say she is scared, on account of when she was a kid she had got into a accident. But ain't no accident or nothing could ever be able to stop me from wanting the power to drive. To get away ... to go somewhere else ... anywhere else.

Mami say maybe it was that old *Next Car* game that got us wishing for cars, but I know that ain't it at all. I been watching Mami waiting on others to take her places for my whole life and I want to be able to take myself and her to wherever we want to go. I never wanna have to depend on no one.

I watch out my window today waiting for Aunt Big Luzzy. She got a car and she say that she going to pick us up and take us to *Jones Beach*.

I don't really like the beach ... something about the sand and not being able to see my feet in the water and steppin' on them shells just ain't for me. But at *Jones Beach*, in section 6, they got a pool. It cost fifty cents to get in, but once you pay they put a stamp on your hand and if we fast enough that stamp got enough ink for one more person to rub on. Mami say it's like getting two for the price of one. My sister Ana say that it is stealing and my mami say, "How can you steal a pool?" and that God will forgive us on account of he wants our family to be able to buy ice cream that day just like everyone else.

When my aunt Luzzy car rolls down our block I feel like the luckiest girl in the world. Mami, Ana, Ben, Danny and me run downstairs and load into her car.

My aunt Luzzy don't like to put on the air conditioner on account of she say that her car is gonna overheat. But no matter how hot it be in that car the idea of *Jones Beach* pool makes my cheeks hurt from smiling so much.

Poolside is the best place in the world. I ain't never learn't how to swim but I sit with my legs in the water, watching everybody have fun and feeling so good. Sun shining on me and everybody is just happy.

I spot this pretty lady and she got on a lot of makeup and I think that's how I'm gonna be when I grow up.

When it's hot enough I step in the shallow side. Four feet is my max, just enough to keep my neck out and my hair dry. And I can breathe.

In the crowd of people the lady with the make up stands out like a shiny diamond.

I rubberneck to keep my eyes on her and learn her classiness but I bump into somebody—

"Excuse me, Mister, I ain't see you there."

I walk to move around him, but he kinda move the same way and keep blocking. I look up at him. It is a white-haired man and just then I realize that he blocking me on purpose. I go to move around him again, and that's when he touches me in my private parts.

He squeeze me between my legs twice and he walk away like it ain't never happen, and I-I-I don't know what to do. My face feels red from shame, and I look around and wonder if anybody seen't it.

I look over at the classy lady, and then to my two brothers who are doing belly flops into the pool.

Ain't nobody see it. And I-I-I

Get from the pool and land back by Mami and my aunt

Luzzy's pool chairs.

I dry myself off and use my bed sheet to hide myself from the sun ... to hide myself from the old man ... to hide myself from the world ... to hide myself from myself.

I lay there and wonder how much longer we will have to stay and wish that I could be back in my room, watching the world from my window.

7 CRIME WAVE

The world outside of Brownsville ain't much different from the world inside ... except what you expec' from it. Something happen to you outside of Brownsville—is like a pop quiz at school on the day after you been absent. Inside, is like the state exam you been preparing for all year. So which one is harder?

From the minute you start walking through them projects you learn you gotta keep your head and eyes up to make sure ain't nobody gonna hit you on the head with a bottle or something.

I heard about this woman, come home from a hospital with her newborn baby boy in a carriage. Scissor came down and that baby was no more. I ain't see that happen. I just heard about it. But you hear about a lot of things you know is true.

I think the worst thing I ever heard was a couple of years back at *Our Lady of Mercy* church our priest had got stabbed a whole bunch of times for the collection plate. He survived but he left the church and a new priest took his place. Wasn't too long before the new one got shot in another robbery and one of our nuns, Sister Joan, had got raped too.

Enough to make you think maybe being a Christian ain't the way to go after all. Made Mami take her picture of Jesus Christ down from our kitchen.

I seen Sister Joan every Easter and Christmas and at my sister Ana's confirmation and my brothers' communions, but after that Mami say she ain't need to be bothered with me taking religious classes. Mami say God is prolly closer to us on the twelfth floor than he could be at a one-level church.

All I know is I wasn't never gonna have them same pictures that my sister got. Nice white dress, lace around her head, rosary in her hands, knelt on a pew and praying to God. So I hope the *"Our Father"* prayer is the only one I will need to know to get into heaven.

Crack is getting worse than ever these days and ain't no time of day that you could come into our lobby and not recognize a drug deal going down. Not no big ones, just a whole lotta nickel and dime-ing. Enough to make me see that cops must be real stupid, 'cause if they wanna catch somebody all they gotta do is stand around and wait.

Drug deals, shootings …

This one time this lady named Saida, she was screaming real loud and I could hear her from three floors up and across the hall. She was screaming *"Me lo mataron!"*— means "they killed him!"

They had shot her husband Chong—he wasn't Chinese or nothing, they just called him that 'cause he got slanty eyes, but he's really Puerto Rican. Chong used to buy and sell jewelry from his apartment, just like they do at the pawn shops. He was always walking around flashing some cash and ready to buy.

They say Chong prolly knew the guys that killed him on account of he opened up his door. They shot him right in front of his whole family, a whole bunch of times.

Alls I could think is that he should a known't better. Even if you getting robbed you can't make no sudden moves. Just gotta give them what they want and hope they run away.

I learnt that when I was eight years old, or maybe I was seven. Me and my mami was coming home from buying food on Belmont Avenue. Mami had one bag a groceries. A head of lettuce, couple of tomatoes, a two-liter *Pepsi* soda, and a bag of rice that could last us the whole week.

It was the middle of a summer day, and I was so happy 'cause on the bottom of that bag was also a new set of *jacks* Mami bought me. My hands was big enough to do tensies. And I was better at it than my two brothers and my sister.

Me and Mami was in our lobby waiting on the elevator. Only one of the two elevators was working that day. I spot this dude. Ain't never seen him before. This is how I know you ain't gotta be older than eight years old in Brownsville to know that something ain't right about a dude you ain't never seen't before.

He black and tall and skinny with a ostrich head. He wearing glasses and a red African tribal shirt, make him look like he gonna talk like a Rastafarian, even though his hair is short to his head.

We get on the elevator. I think Mami rather be polite than show that she think something is wrong about him. She wait for him to press his number first and he press the number nine before Mami show that we going up to twelve.

I have seen't my mother suspicious before. She always wait on other people to press they floor first. If they press fourteen, Mami press twenty, even though we live on twelve. She don't wanna have to turn her back on nobody she don't know. She don't want nobody following us into our home. She wanna keep it safe.

Elevator doors is closing and crazy Miss Stark come running through the lobby door, holding her arm out and running toward the elevator, so fast I think the pick might finally fall from her afro. Mami is quick to press the "Door Open" button for her but instead of saying "thank you" Miss Stark say what she always say.

"Hi, Hi, Hi, how you doing?" That's all she say (fact, Miss Stark is kinda famous for saying it), and she keep saying it, with a twitch of her nose in between every time.

Poor Miss Stark seem like a broken record to me. But Mami know she had a nervous breakdown after her husband died in Vietnam and she raising her two boys all alone, and so she just keep answering her saying, "Good." "Good." "Good." "Good." "Good."

We ride up eight floors of "Hi, hi, hi, how you doings"

before Miss Stark finally steps off. And when she do, it's just me, my mami and that dude that we never seen't before. Seem like a long time before we reach just one more floor up. Me and Mami ain't saying nothing but we vibing the same thing, and I am watching for any suspicious moves.

Ninth floor, the elevator door opens and the dude creeps out. Real slow, light on his first foot, like he ain't got no real place to go. Still I am happy that he making his move, and his move is away from us. As the elevator door closes I could feel me and Mami breathe out at the same time. Like we been waiting to exhale from the moment we got into that elevator with him.

That's when I seen't his hand push the elevator door back open. He has a gun in his other hand, I know now it was a .38 snub nose. But back then, just look like it was made from the same metal they use to build train tracks, and he say, "Your money or your life."

My mami ain't make no sudden moves. She just stepped a little bit in front of me and like her hand was in slow motion she handed him her last five dollars. He took it fast but Mami held it for a extra second and asked him, "Why you robbing me? I'm poor."

His gun hand was shaking, pointing at us. He put his other hand on Mami's chest and patted her down, to make sure she wasn't hiding no money there, and then he left.

Mami pressed the "Door Close" button a million times and as soon as we got to the twelfth floor, she start running out before the door was open enough to let her through. Fast as she could and screaming. It dawned on me that she was afraid that the dude was gonna beat us up the stairs and do something worse to us.

Once we was safe inside our apartment, we was looking out the window thinking that we might see the dude and point him out to one of them drug dealers we know, that might have a gun, and give the dude something to answer to. But we didn't see him and before long I reached into the grocery bag that Mami left on the floor by our front door, and took out my *jacks*. So happy to still have them. I start playing and I say to myself but out loud so I could hear it and believe it, "Ain't nothing wrong. Ain't nothing wrong."

Mami put the groceries away. The soda was like Mami, shaken and ready to explode. Then she start cleaning our already clean apartment. And then she started crying. Complaining about her life to Jesus Christ. She ask him why he give her this life? I was more okay with the robbery than seeing my mami cry like that.

When Mami seen't me starting to cry too, she showed me her change was in her other front pocket. The one hidden by her bag of groceries. She had a whole bunch a change in that pocket, was almost four dollars. She start trying to make me feel better saying he ain't really rob us after all, and that he was so stupid.

Then she just started ranking on the dude, making fun of his ugly shirt and his ostrich head. She say he ain't even take her groceries and that I still had my *jacks*. She say that he was running somewhere to get away, and we here safe, clean, playing and with food to eat. And that made me laugh and feel a lot better.

My mother always found ways to make us feel better.

8 FIRST KISS

Today, like every other Sunday, I hang out of my window waiting to see if any of the Puerto Rican women sit on the benches just outside of the building. 'Cause as soon as they do, I'm gonna tell Mami, hoping that she decides to join them. 'Cause that means that I get to go outside too.

I can walk to my junior high school but other than that I still ain't allowed outside alone in Brownsville.

My brothers, Benjamin and Danny, been allowed to go outside alone for a while now. They mostly play basketball and *skelly*. And my sister, Ana, is always working at a store in Bushwick ever since she got her working papers.

Mami thinks that hanging out can't lead to nothing good round here. And I know that she is right. When Ana first started going out alone she used to wear her purse round her neck. Then she got her purse snatched and came home shaking and crying with a red neck. Then, Benjamin went out and came back to our hallway with a dude that he thought did it. The dude was shaking and crying more than Ana was. He told Ana to look through the peephole to identify him, but it wasn't him so Benjamin just let the guy go.

Wait! I see Sandra Garcia outside on the benches. Sandra Garcia is fifteen years old but her body is as big as most grown women's is. She is so ugly that the boys call her San-drac, like *Dracula*. Her eyes are too close together, and her eyebrows connect. The end of her nose looks like it is attached to the top of her lip. And her teeth are bucked, because she still sucks her thumb. Sandra live with her grandmother on account of her mami is a prostitute—that's what some people say.

When she first came to live around here, we was both still little.

We were chasing each other around the column in the lobby and she changed direction on me and her buck teeth hit me right at the top of my lip. Made me bleed. A lot. I still got the scar. I like Sandra—but most people don't. If they don't call her San-drac, they call her *Lurch*. These are not nice things to say, especially because the same boys all talk about her body in the exact opposite way.

I see Sandra's grandmother.

"Mami, Sandra's grandmother is outside!" I call over to the kitchen.

Mami sticks her head out of the kitchen window, and looks across the building at me before saying, "Okay, go get your *jellies* on. We will go outside."

I run to my closet and put on my white sneakers instead of my *jellies*. I hate to show my toes, because feet are ugly. Even the prettiest feet are ugly to me.

By the time we get downstairs there are two other Puerto Rican women there too. Saida Ramos from the ninth floor and Jackie Nuñez from the fourteenth floor with her only daughter, Fat Chana.

Chana is way too old to be wanting to hang out with her mother. She like twenty or something—but I'm also pretty sure that don't nobody else wanna hang out with her on account of she so fat. It is too bad that she is so fat too, 'cause she got a real pretty face and nice curly hair, and light brown eyes.

Mami always be telling her that she should try to lose some weight because she is so pretty. I know that might sound mean, but believe me when I say that Mami says it in the nicest way possible and Fat Chana takes it in the best way possible. They are friends.

"Hi, Sandra."

"Hi, Elaine. Ask your mother if you can come with me to *Johnny's* bodega to get some sunflower seeds and *Bon Ton* potato chips."

I hate when Sandra ask me things like that, because she know that my mother is surely gonna say NO, and then I am gonna be embarrassed because I ain't so little that I shouldn't be able to walk to the corner. *Johnny's* is not even a half a block away.

"You ask her." I say.

Mami is talking real serious with Fat Chana, prolly telling her that she could come over and exercise in our apartment later if she wants. Mami is always offering her that, but Chana don't never come by.

I don't even want to look while Sandra is interrupting Mami. If I look, she just gonna give me a dirty look and think that it was my idea. If I don't look she just prolly gonna think that Sandra is way stupider than me for even asking.

"She said yes." Sandra says. "I told her I got a dollar for the stuff."

"She did not ... you lying! You trying to get me in trouble! Mami did you say that I could go get some seeds with Sandra?"

"Yes. *Nena*. Go 'head. Just come right back. I'm timing you." Mami points at her wrist even though she ain't got a watch.

Before Mami was finished with her sentence I turn't my back to her and started walking fast and away in case she change her mind at the last second.

"Wait up!" Sandra say.

Me and Sandra are just out of sight of Mami at the benches when we see two Puerto Rican boys on bikes that is way too small for them. They prolly stole them.

They coming toward us and I know one of them from school. He used to go to my old elementary school before he moved. His name is Roberto Mendez. I musta written his name down ten thousand times on my notebook hoping that he would notice me, but he never did.

He was in the Special Ed class, so he was prolly too stupid

to notice. One day, in the lunchroom, Crysta Robins passed him a note that said that I liked him and his face turn't red, and he started laughing. But he still ain't say nothing. I told Crysta Robins thanks for that on account of him laughing like that make me realize that he had *Bugs Bunny* teeth, and so I didn't like him anymore … even though I really did.

Roberto didn't pay no attention to me then—just the same way he ain't paying no attention to me now. He just watching Sandra shake her booty with every step she take.

The other boy—I ain't never seen him before. Must not be from around here. He Latino but he got beady eyes like he Chinese and he got greasy hair. His skin is dark like an Indian and he ain't nothing much to look at compared to Roberto. He not totally ugly, but he not nothing much to look at.

If Mami see me with these two boys, she not never gonna let me leave her side again.

They pedal slow alongside us until we get to *Johnny's* store.

Then Roberto say, "Let's keep walking. Just around the corner on Belmont. See if the candy store is open."

It is Sunday after five p.m. and I know that the candy store gots to be closed by now. Five o'clock on a Sunday and all the gates on all the stores is down for sure, especially the candy store. Well it ain't really a store. It is just a little booth with a little sliding bullet proof window big enough to let you see the face of the man selling you candy inside it.

"The candy store ain't opened."

"What, are you scared? You act like you a baby or something. It might be open," says Sandra. Then she say something else in Roberto's ear that make me know she making fun of me. Make me wanna say shut up San-drak! You the one who is still sucking your thumb like a baby—NOT ME. But she would prolly knock me out if I said that, so I just stay quiet and feel my ears burning red hot.

"You probably never even kissed a boy." Sandra says.

I am looking at Roberto and wishing that he was rapping to me instead of to Sandra.

"I did kiss a boy." I lied. "In Philadelphia."

And then we start walking again. Roberto and his friend

rolling beside us.

"You ain't never kissed a boy before. If you did, then I dare you to kiss him!"

Sandra took her thumb out of her mouth just long enough to point at Roberto's friend.

I used to pretend that my *Ken* doll was Roberto and I was *Barbie*—and I would put their lips together—

"I dare you. Kiss him!"

I look at him and feel like I am up against a wall, but he looking at me like he wish that I would and—it makes me feel good. I smile a weak smile and think that he not that bad after all. He actually kinda okay. I ain't really pay no attention to him before on account of I was hoping on Roberto, but he's not ugly at all.

"I'm Carlos," he says.

We round the corner onto Belmont Avenue and just like I said, all the gates is down on the stores. The streets is empty except for the four of us.

"I dare you."

Sandra start kissing Roberto and her mouth is open and her tongue is moving all around and grossing me out. I look at Carlos, feeling real stupid.

I walk closer to his bike … Carlos's bike. I close my eyes… and I think about Mami's soap operas and how kissing go on all the time … like it wasn't nothin' and so … I kiss him—on the mouth. And all in three seconds, it feels stupid and weird and sloppy and … good.

The yanking of my braid make me open my eyes.

"You slut!" My brother Benjamin's voice echoes down the gated alleyway.

He grabs me by my hair, and slams me against the gates of the *99 cent* store. I am too scared and embarrassed to feel the pain from his yank. But I could see some of my hair has come out of my head and is still in his clenched fist and that one of my sneakers flung off and now lays at my big-head brother's feet.

I run as fast as I can back to my building, leaving my favorite sneaker on Belmont Avenue. I am feeling the back of my head hoping that I don't got a bald spot. That will surely remind everybody of this forever.

Everybody is going to be talking about this!

Everybody is going to make fun of me!

Sandra is never gonna stop telling people how my brother Benjamin slapped me upside my head, and called me a slut. And how I kissed a boy that I had just met and that I am stupid. A big stupid baby with a big bald spot, whose father was on drugs.

Benjamin ain't never gonna believe that I ain't never done nothing like that before, and I can't blame him.

"You better run!"

I look back at Benjamin. He let go of my hair from his right hand and he holding his basketball under his left arm and laughing at me. I can't hear what he saying to Sandra, but I know it ain't nothing nice. Prolly calling her *Lurch* and Sandrac. He prolly saying that her mother is a prostitute crack head and that's why her grandmother gotta raise her.

And even though everybody thinks that's the truth don't nobody ever say that out loud. They is some lines that you just can't cross. But Benjamin don't care. Benjamin don't care about nothing and nobody!

Roberto and Carlos is pedaling them little boy bikes as fast as they can. Away from my brother that I used to call Big Head and now everybody just calls Big Ben, 'cause he so tall. Too tall to be knocking me around for sure.

I hate him! I hate his guts!

I wait by my apartment door. I wait knowing that Benjamin is prolly telling Mami and all the Puerto Ricans beside her all about it. Once one Puerto Rican knows then they all gonna know.

Don't matter how much I cry, ain't nobody gonna feel sorry for me.

I think about my sister Ana coming home from high school last year and telling Mami that she kissed a boy for the first time. His name was Joey Espinosa and she even had a picture of him. He was cute and even though I made fun of my sister, I really wished that the same thing would happen to me one day.

But instead Sandra Garcia dared me to kiss a boy named Carlos with greasy hair and beady eyes in front of a *99 cent* store. Roberto will never ever like me in a million years. He probably gonna tell every boy in Brownsville not to ever like me 'cause my brother Benjamin will kill them if they even think about it.

When I was little, Mami used to read me *Cinderella* every day. Like ten times a day. I always wished of being like *Cinderella*—going to a ball then running away and missing my shoe and then being happily ever after ... *Cinderella* was lucky ... on account of she ain't have no stupid brother.

9 NEVER RAN

My sister, Ana, she real smart. She about to graduate from *Brooklyn Tech* High School. Tech stands for technical. She go to school and she got a job too. She even saved enough money to go on a vacation. My sister's plan was to come back with a suntan, black as she could get. Ana is lucky that way, she could get real dark on account of she start out a little brown anyway.

When I catch a suntan, it ain't nothing but red and patchy. All my freckles come out, and within two days I'm ashy and peeling. It's like lifting dried up *Elmer's*, and having to scratch off what don't lift right away. Ana gonna be like a bronze queen in her white cap and gown walking down her school auditorium aisle to get her high school diploma.

Well, that was the plan, but yesterday her school called and told Mami that they wasn't gonna let my sister walk down the aisle, on account of she ain't return't her math textbook yet. They say she gotta return it or pay one hundred dollars. Well, Mami wasn't even trying to hear that, yo. At first she tried to come out her face at them, but then she decided to be mad at my sister instead. My mami was going on and on in her usual pattern, first mad and yelling, and then sad and crying. She was saying how Ana need to graduate 'cause Mami ain't never graduate herself, and that she need to be able to take pictures to put in the album.

I could just imagine how my sister musta been crying on the other end of that phone line. 'Bout an hour later, Ana called back and said that she spoke to her friend, Lisa, from school. Lisa was gonna meet us at the number three Rockaway Avenue train stop. She'll be on the platform, and we need to bring that math book over there to her. Did I say we? 'Cause I meant me.

Whatever happened to Mami not wanting me outside alone?

Mami didn't care about her own rules or if I would be late to my homeroom or my first period algebra class with Mr. Coye, even when I said I got a test. She said my brothers couldn't do it, on account of they take the Double L train to their high school, and high school is more important than junior high school—even if I do got the meanest math teacher in the whole school giving me the hardest test in the whole school.

We got two train stations that border Brownsville, both is about ten blocks from where I live, but they in total opposite directions. The double L train—that's the one my brothers take. It's the one straight up on Sutter Avenue.

When you walk to the double L train, you gotta walk ten blocks straight up Sutter Avenue, but you gotta cross the street after seven blocks so that you don't have to walk by the methadone clinic. Methadone is the medicine people take when they trying to get off a heroin. I think it comes in a pink bottle, 'cause I remember when Mami told us not to touch this thing that she had in the refrigerator for Papi. Papi didn't leave the bedroom for a lot of days. I could hear him suffering. Mami said he was sick that whole time while that medicine was in the refrigerator. I can't believe that Papi was ever one of those people by the methadone clinic. They be all lined up hanging down the walls, waiting for their methadone medicine. Everything hanging. Their clothes hanging off their bodies. Their skin hanging off their bones. Their bodies hanging down the brick walls. Their drool hanging from they lips. I'm not scared of them, 'cause they all move so slow. Like scratching your Afro take three minutes for their hanging hand to reach their hanging head.

The number three train, is our other train. You gotta walk straight up Rockaway Avenue for that. Or you could take the B60 Bus, but by the time you get done waiting for the B60 Bus to take you the ten blocks to get to the number three train, you may as well had walked it. Mami says it's good exercise.

We learning about all kinds of angles in math class. The shortest distance. I think about it all the time. What's the shortest way I could get to anywhere? What buildings could I cut through to make it all go faster? But usually, I just be taking the long way, 'cause that way there be more people out. It's just safer.

Out the building. On my way to return the text book. I keep my head up to make sure ain't nobody gonna hit me on the head with a bottle or something. They be throwing all kinds a things out the window round here.

I leave the building and pass the Chinese hole-in-the-wall restaurant where fried rice and chicken wings fly out the door for $3.25. Then the numbers joint where Mami and my *abuela* play their numbers every day. *Johnny's* store is on the corner. Most of the refrigerators is filled with 40-ounce bottles of *Old English* beer. No matter when you go in there, you see somebody getting a 40 ounce of *Old English*, a pack of sunflower seeds, and a couple of cups in a bag to go with the loose cigarettes you could buy for ten cents each—on account of most of the time, people don't got enough money to buy a whole pack of cigarettes.

Pass the bus stop. People waiting for the B60. It's crowded. Some of them people ain't no way they gonna get on the next bus. I rather walk than be still in the cold.

Block two. Papi's old school, P.S. 125, which closed last year. The building is all boarded up, but they still got a playground there where don't nobody go.

All the times I used to go there with my father, but I still can't help but to remember it more for the fact that that's where Mami's friend from the fourth floor of our building, Gladys, almost got raped a couple years back.

The doors to the apartments in our building is metal, and the knocker in the middle, that's metal too. When somebody knocks everybody on the floor could hear it. And when they knock loud, then you could hear the echo for floors.

I don't really know what happened with Gladys, but I can remember the knocker pounding on our apartment door. It was to wake my dad up to join the crew that was out looking for the guy who tried to rape Gladys in the playground of Papi's school.

Later I overheard people talking about it in the lobby. They said that Gladys was begging the guy to let her go. She even told him that she had her period. He ripped at her clothes anyway. Then a car stopped and a guy helped her. She was bleeding on account of the guy punched her in the mouth.

A posse of Puerto Rican men came knocking at every Puerto Rican man's door in our building. They all went looking for the homeless bum that Gladys described. Papi took his aluminum baseball bat, and we all stayed up staring out the window. It was four o'clock in the morning when they came walking back up the block. Mami scream't out the window like she was waking up the sun, "Did you get him?"

"No."

Gladys shoulda been more careful. No girl should be out there when it's dark.

Now 8:30 in the morning, I know I gotta walk across the street every now and again to make sure ain't nobody following me. That's just common sense.

Block five. I see this real tall black dude. He looking at me, kinda how I look at Mami's fried chicken fresh out the frying pan. I could tell that he like me a lot. He got a little mustache and must be older, but I can't tell how old 'cause black don't crack.

I try to look ugly, but he don't care. I shouldn't had worn these stretch *Jeanjer* jeans. These are my favorite jeans. They faded in between the pleats of the stretches, and I know how they make my shape look, especially right after they washed.

He staring me down. Shoulder to shoulder now, and as he pass me, he say, "Sexy."

I walk faster, a short light-skinned dude in front of me turns around to see what was sexy to the tall dude. I walk faster, turning around to look over my shoulder to make sure that the tall dude ain't turn around to follow me.

He don't. He just keep going on his way. I feel mad and cold. The wind comes right through my jean pleats and burns my legs. My nose is running and my eyes is tearing. I got a patch on my eye today 'cause I got *Conjunctivitis*. But I'm wearing white sunglasses so don't nobody could see my patch unless they really looking.

Argh!

"Shut the fuck up bitch!"

The little dude that was in front of me grabbed me. He got his hand around my shoulder and pressing on my neck tight. My eyes is tearing but I ain't crying. I'm just trying to think. Think about anything but what's gonna happen to me if he get me to where there ain't nobody around.

He can't drag me into no building back staircase, 'cause then too many people could see. We already passed Gladys's park and we walking away from it, and I'm real glad about that. I wish I seen't that tall dude now 'cause then if he like me, maybe he would help me. But he not here no more. It's just me and this little light skinned dude.

The tears from the cold is mixing with the new tears just starting from being scared. We pass a busy bus stop. Another one for the B60. Can anyone see my tears? They ain't gotta look real hard on account of my glasses is half off my face hanging down.

The black girl at the bus stop. She's real dark skin't and pretty. She's wearing a black leather blazer and skirt with boots. Her skin nearly as black and shiny as her coat. She knows I'm crying 'cause I lower my head to try to stop his choke, and my glasses fall off my face. She and me is locking eyes, but her eyes don't blink—like she dead with her eyes open, and she seen this before. My eyes don't blink neither, hoping she show me a sign. The B60 screeches to a stop right in front of her, and other people run to make it and huddle behind her. She staring hard. The bus doors open, and she steps her boot onto the first step. She holds on to the rail, still staring without blinking. And I could see a thought blink through her eyes. She gets on that bus, and as it pulls away, I wonder if she still staring at me. I wonder if she gonna tell the bus driver. If she too scared, like me, or if she just don't care.

But me and this dude, we just keep walking.

"Mister, please let me go."

But he don't say nothing.

"Mister, please let me go. I not gonna say nothing."

But he don't say nothing.

"Mister, please—"

And he say, "Shut the fuck up, I got a gun."

And all I keep thinking is, if he got a gun, then he would prolly take it out, or make me feel it. He prolly ain't got no gun. People be fronting like that all the time. You gots to fake it sometimes, so people could fear you.

"If you gotta gun, then you should take it out and show it to me."

And he say, "If I take it out, then I'm gonna shoot you."

I just keep thinking he prolly don't got no gun.

But then I remember this tall dark chocolate dude wearing all leather last summer. He looked so fly, he was bopping that cool walk, and then his bop turned into a hop. I ain't even hear the pap from the gun that shot him. I was staring at him walking and admiring his gear, but somehow I missed it all. Is that what happened with the girl at the bus stop and me? She was staring at me, the way I was staring at him and then he just start saying, "I been shot. I been shot".

He grabs me tighter. Choking me. I just keep thinking, if this dude gonna shoot me now, then he prolly gonna shoot me after he done with me. I ain't got nothing to rob.

Three more blocks to the number three train station. That train is on Livonia and Rockaway and it run all above ground over there. And don't nobody walk over there, 'cause even in the brightest of sunshines it be dark as night. He chokes me harder and we cross the street, away from the people at the next bus stop. I know where we walking to…under the train. The buildings is abandoned just past the liquor store.

As we walk faster, it feel like the people is whipping by, hard as the wind. Some of them is looking at me and some of them is not, but they all doing the same thing. They all doing nothing.

"Mister, please. I got my period." I ain't know why I thought that that was gonna make a difference, but I just keep thinking about Gladys, and what she said, and what she musta been thinking.

It's like, I'm scared but at the same time I'm calm. Like I know if I don't be calm, then he not gonna be calm. But if he get me underneath that number three train, he prolly gonna rape me, and then if he really gotta gun, he gonna shoot me. If I gonna get shot. I might as well get shot before I get raped. I might as well let myself get shot in front of people, so that after I get shot somebody could help me. Once the dude shoots me, he'll run away, and then people will help me.

We walking and walking, and I could clearly see his destination now. I was right. The train is half a block away. On the left side is all buildings where people live, but on the right by the liquor store, ain't nothing but boarded up windows and empty lots where heroin addicts sit on old tires getting high.

There's a newsstand right before the number three train entrance, and it's packed. It always be packed. And I just keep thinking if I gonna be helped by anyone, it's gonna be by somebody over there. Somebody that works somewhere they gotta take a train to get to. Somebody that reads on they way to work.

As we come up on that newsstand, I eye this real tall dude. He much bigger than the guy that got me. My stare is burning a hole through his burgundy du-rag. As he pass his 50 cents to pay for his *Daily News* newspaper, he see me. He smile, and he see me. He notice what's going on. He see me! As the hold around my neck gets stronger, I'm afraid to say the words out loud. If this little dude gotta gun, he gonna shoot me and everybody else around me. So I mouth the words, as a flood of scared tears that can't never be mistaken for tears from the cold pour down my face. There's a mess of snot on my lips as they silently say, "HELP." As clear as I can, but without making a sound, "HELP." The dude see me. He see me…

But he not doing nothing. And as we pass him, I could see the liquor store, and I know around this corner is the abandoned buildings and lots. As we round the corner, his grip on my neck stiffens and so do my hands around my little blue book bag carrying my sister's text book. I need to get that book to Lisa, so my sister could graduate for us. I hold my book bag tight as I can, and I start swinging and swinging and swinging and swinging.

BLACK OUT. Like time was vacuumed into a tunnel with no light at either end.

As I started to come to. I could barely see. Blurry colors streaked by my blinks. I couldn't feel no pain. I was thinking that this is dead. Maybe when we die, we stay here, dead on this earth. Just able to watch blurry colors through tears, never able to feel or move. I could feel nothing. Not even the cold.

And that's when I saw the dude that had grabbed me. He wasn't beside me no more. He was on the ground. I could just barely make it out, but I could see his face. It was moving from left to right guided by the punches from somebody's hands. They was punching him and scratching him. His face moved with them punches and I couldn't say nothing. But my whole being was rooting for that puncher like me and Mami did in the final round of the *Rocky* movie. I was so embarrassed at the movie theater as Mami's hands punched with Rocky's, but now I felt the way she musta was feeling.

The train roared above me, and I kept thinking that my sister's friend, Lisa, was gonna be there on that platform, waiting for that book. Waiting for me. Wondering if I'm ever gonna come. Leaving when she think I won't. Mad as hell that she gonna be late, and that I wasted her time. Sorry that she agreed to do my sister the favor. I just kept thinking about my sister's book, and then of Mami's photo album that need the pictures of my sister walking down that aisle as she graduates from *Brooklyn Tech*.

I looked around for my book bag, and I seen't it…right by the train station entrance. It was a half a block away from where I am. It was at the last place I remembered being, before

I blacked out or died. I got up to go get my book bag, but my body wasn't moving. I must be dead. And I looked down at the dude's face and at them hands that was punching him and scratching him…

And that's when I realized…that's when I realized that them was my hands.

I looked at my hands and willed them to stop. Willed my body to realign with my mind. I got up to go get my book bag, and as I picked it up, I could feel the cold creeping up behind me. Was it the cold or was it him—ready to pounce on me and drag me to the drug den?

I looked back. He was running away. He wasn't running. He was limping and holding his head. And I ain't feel dead no more, or like I was rooting for Rocky. I felt like I was Rocky. Like I won. I did this. All by myself. I beat a dude up. I ain't never been in no fight before, 'cause I ain't never look for trouble, and I ain't never felt strong neither, but I do now. I feel so strong. Like they ain't nobody ever gonna hurt me. Like I know when my mind stop, my body gonna take over, and I ain't got nothing to ever worry about. Not here and not anywhere.

I know why I had to bring my sister's book. This big text book. I know why I had to bring it.

People from Bedford Stuyvesant, they got this saying. They say they from "Bed Stuy, Do or Die." Me, I'm from Brownsville and we got a saying too. "Brownsville, Brownsville, Never Ran, Never Will."

10 LUCKY

Of all the people I have ever known, my brother Benjamin (aka Big Head) is the luckiest. Sometimes, he finds dollars somebody else lost, right where he stands. Not a week goes by that Benjamin don't be bragging about finding something or other. I ain't never consider myself lucky like that before today.

I been listening to *92-WKTU* station on the radio all summer long.

Been waiting for the song of the day to play. Trying to be caller number 92 so I could win. I dial a thousand times—I usually stop trying when I hear the DJ come back on the radio with his winner. He say, "Caller number 92. What's the song of the day?"

That's when I hang up and wish that I could have dialed faster and was any kind of lucky like my big-head brother.

But today, I was fast enough! And the song of the day was my very favorite song "*My Adidas*" by my very favorite rap group *Run-DMC*. The song was still playing when the DJ answered, so I ain't think I was the winner, but then he said it: I won!

Most of the time, the prize is ninety-two dollars but today the prize makes me the luckiest caller on the luckiest day of all time. Two tickets to go see *Run-DMC* at *Madison Square Garden*!

I's jumping for joy.

The DJ asked me to hold on. Then while I was waiting for him to come back to the phone, I could hear my own voice coming out of the radio like it was a dream. And I gotta pinch myself to know that this is really happening to me! I listened to what musta been a recording saying everything that we had just said on the phone, but this time, it was coming through the radio's speakers. I was so happy for myself that I could cry!

I won tickets to *Madison Square Garden*.

I had heard of "The Garden" many times on account of thass where the *New York Knicks* play all they basketball games.

My brothers have talked 'bout going there and being in the nose-bleed seats. They took the train to 34th Street to get there and so I know how I will go.

But I also know that I gonna have to sneak out to go.

I call my one friend from school, Mari Santiago and ask her if she could lie and say she got a party that she want me to go to.

Mari Santiago hangs up on me, but I tell my mami the lie and she believes me.

On the day of the concert, Mami watches me from the window as I walk across the street to Mari Santiago's building.

I sneak out the back of the building and walk to the train station.

I duck under the turnstile and take the number 3 train to *Madison Square Garden*.

Madison Square Garden—is so big! Excited *Run DMC* fans are everywhere!

I find Will Call and, even though she looking at me like I shouldn't be alone, the counter lady hands me my ticket.

Madison Square Garden is so big that you gotta take a escalator just to get to where your seat is at. I open the doors to the entrance of the arena. There are a million people just like me. Except most of them are black—it's like the Brownsville *Langston Hughes* Projects got turned upside down and emptied in one place, right here and we all here for the same reason … to enjoy the best words ever put to music.

I been writing raps ever since Papi left. My first lyrics were to *Run-DMC's "Sucker MC"* beat. Don't nobody really want to listen to me do it, but I got three whole spiral notebooks full of words that I wrote. Ninety-nine pages each with nothing but rhymes come straight out of my head. My favorite is one where I am a superhero. I replace the thugs and the drugs with hugs.

That's how I feel right now! Like a superhero getting hugged by all this electricity around me.

I find my way to my seat just as the lights go down. Flashbulbs pop everywhere, and everybody is standing. I stand too but I still can't see over the people in front of me...but I could hear them. I could hear *Run* and *DMC*, both from Hollis, Queens before even a beat drops. It's just *Run's* magical voice:

"I'm the King of Rock, there is none higher
Sucker MCs, should call me sire
To burn my kingdom, you must use fire
And I won't stop rocking till I retire"

The music plays to back him up, as his DJ is lit up behind them. I could see DJ *Jam Master Jay* because he is on a platform raised above them. He is wearing black leather pants, untied *Adidas*, a gray sweatshirt and headphones underneath his black hat. His turntables are lit up all around him.

Run jumps up on the platform and I finally catch a glimpse of the most talented man that ever walked this earth! I wish I could show him my rhymes.

The music is so loud that even the excited crowd around me can't overwhelm it. I feel people moving all around me, and all I could think is how lucky I am to be here.

Then I feel somebody on my hand. A touch becomes a pull and a push until I tumble to the ground. But this is not an accidental fall.

I am dragged from where my seat was to the area where I first stood taking it all in. I keep trying to pull myself up, but I am being pulled back, kicked down. More than one kick at a time and I soon understand that these actions come upon me with purpose.

Either gold rings, or brass knuckles punch at my face.

Three, four, five hands; six, seven, eight legs to every part of my body. I try to protect my face, like my brothers Benjamin and Danny always do when they play fight. I crunch my body small as I could get it and just take the beating. I think about my aunts and uncles and grandmother catching a beating from the grandfather I never knew. I think about my father.

Then just as fast as they came around me, they all just moved away ... all at once. Like a swarm of pigeons on a crumb of bread.

I felt somebody take my hand and pull me up—a man!

A moment to feel the fear, and prepare for more before I realize that he is pulling me up to help me. He was not a part of what just happened ... whatever had just happened.

My head is so heavy, like it suddenly is too heavy for the rest of my body to carry.

I find my way to the Exit sign and the doorway that leads me to the now empty hallway. *Madison Square Garden* is more like a circle than a square. I follow the hallway around until I see the signs for the restrooms. A couple is running past me to get to their seats and they stop and stare at me, like, why am I leaving?

That's what I thought they were thinking until—

Inside of the bathroom, I look in the mirror and I know why they were staring at me like that.

I ain't even recognize myself. My right eye is all swell't up, and I am struggling to open it. When I do, the round brown that used to be the inside of my eye ain't round no more. Ain't no shape at all. I can't even see the white of my eye. Under it, my cheek is bleeding so bad I can't tell where the cut starts.

The more I look, the more my face changes, for the worse.

I ain't have nothing to rob. Nothing. Nothing of value except for that lucky winning ticket that somehow I still have in my hand. It is crumpled now ... like my face.

So why? Why did they beat me?

Because I lied to Mami?

Because I ain't never made my communion?

Then, I know.

See, you hear about them gang initiations all the time…the

ones where people is beat down randomly ... but you don't never think you gonna be the person catching that random beatdown. So random that it just feel UNLUCKY. Cursed even.

The one time I do something and go somewhere I ain't supposed to, I think, God was there to punish me. Them was soldiers, out to get their colors and get with a family, that did this. I seen it before! I seen it plenty! But never from the inside.

Suddenly I ain't care about listening to *Run-DMC*. I feel like *Dorothy* after the tornado in the *Wizard of Oz*, wishing I could be home. First time in a long time that I wished I was home.

On the train back home, I keep my face pointed at the doors and away from anybody sitting. When the train speeds into the tunnels I spot my reflection in the windows of the train door.

Ain't too many good things about me except that before today—before a couple of hours ago—I thought I may be pretty.

I wish I had my pen and spiral notebook right now, cause maybe I would bury my heavy head in it and write something —or maybe I would tear it all apart and wish I never heard a rap song.

If I could write right now, it would write something like this:

It was the best day of my life, or so I thought
It was the worst day of my life, a fight I never fought

Something like that.
Lord, I will never be the same again.
As much as I am feeling bad, all I could think about is my mother, and what she gonna do to me for being somewhere I'm not supposed to be. She gonna say what I already know, "God punished you for lying to me".

I am scared even though my mami ain't never hit me. She ain't never hit none of us, except for Benjamin. When he was little, she always used to slap him upside his head, but he always deserved it. Nowadays, he about a foot and half taller than her, and he still deserve it, so she gotta take a broomstick to him.

Benjamin just be laughing at her, saying, "Ma, you not hurting me. Careful you don't hurt yourself."

That just make Mami madder, but she not really ever trying to hurt him. She just trying to make a point. Then she starts crying. Like it's written in a script somewhere: "Lady starts crying uncontrollably."

Mami prolly never gonna stop crying when she see me. After she get done being mad at me and telling me why God punished me, her mad at me gonna turn to sad for herself. That's when Mami gonna look up and ask God why he doing this to her.

It's dark by the time I get to my building. I run through the half-lit lobby, fast and sneaky like police when they holding a big metal thing that knocks down a door, coming for somebody that's wanted on a warrant.

The cuts on my face hurt from moving, but I don't want nobody to see me.

This building can't keep a secret. I take the back staircase—the place people go to do things they don't wanna be seen doing. Teenagers kissing, thieves changing they shirts so they can't be described in a robbery, drug addicts smoking crack or doing whatever to get some. If somebody gonna see me here in the back staircase, at least I know they not trying to be seen't neither.

I make sounds up the stairs—the closest thing I could get to a whistle on account of my mouth ain't never been able to make a real whistle sound—gotta find some way to let people know I'm coming. Not trying to sneak up on nobody here 'cause scared people could do some crazy things.

You could make as much noise as you want in the back staircase. Only noise you gotta stop yourself from making is one of heavy breathing—that says, "I'm too tired to fight if I need to."

Loud and slow, I walk up twelve flights, deep quiet breaths from my nose so the air don't have to pass my busted lips. Each inhale filling my nose with the stench of piss, like a gas station toilet that ain't been flushed in forever.

I could hear the staircase doors open and people leaving as they hear me walk up. I imagine they are on the other side of that door just waiting on me to pass, so they could get back to they own secret business.

I grip the metal railing so my hands could help my heavy head up.

My nails still have dried blood under them, same as the stains on my sister's beige *Members Only* jacket—that she has screamed at me not to wear a million times. Ana is so sick of me wearing her clothes, she says that I ruin everything I put my hands on. This is the first time that I know she is right. But I wore it because I wanted this day to be as special as it could be.

My ears hurt from her screaming already.

I pull the back door open, creaking like only the back door know how, like it's warning me that something scary is about to happen. Stepping into my twelfth floor hallway, I am wishing hard as I can that my mother ain't home ... but my mother is always home. No job, no education, no husband, just us kids and the apartment paid for by welfare. The food on our plates from food stamps. My mother is only ever cooking, cleaning, crying or exercising—and sometimes all four at the same time.

I slide my key in and fall in as Mami opens the door with me. Ain't no hiding.

My mother grips my wrist with one hand and holds her mouth with the other. Her grip tightens like a handcuff as I try to get to my room. But I can't escape the tears that have already fill't her eyes.

"I'm alright, Mami. Don't worry. It looks worse than it feels," but I am not sure that that is the truth.

Mami boils water to make the coffee that will keep me up all night, as much as I want to go to sleep—to dream a nightmare less scary than my life—but Mami forces her gross caffeinated *Bustelo* into me and warns that I will die in my sleep from the concussion that weighs my head.

I stand there and I want to stop crying, but Mami's crying makes me cry more. My face hurts, but her face got more hurt all over it than mine do. Like it's being stomped on the ground the way mine was, and I am watching every bone in it shift with the pain.

She crying loud and I could barely make out her questions, "*Qué te pasó, nena?* (Who did this to you?)"

The truth came out of me faster than I wanted it to. "Mami, calm down. I'm alright. Wasn't nothing from around here."

When "concert at *Madison Square Garden*" comes out my mouth, Mami's look of hurt changes to the kinda mad she ain't never had before. Mami hurled Spanish curses at me way faster than I could understand.

Her mad gives her super strength and her little five-foot, 100-pound body is dragging my five-foot-five, 125-pound ass to the kitchen.

I think she reaching for her broomstick—but instead she pulls open the refrigerator door, hard like she want to take it off its hinges, like she ain't never gonna need that door again. She take out a stick of cold *Parkay*, and starts smearing it all over my face. My mother swears that a cold stick of imitation butter could help any kinda bruises heal better than anything a pharmacy could provide. She thinks it helps them melt away.

I wish she was feeling sorry for me, but instead she asking me what I did to deserve this beat down. She ain't care 'bout nothing I gotta say so I figure I ain't gots to say another thing. She just keep yelling and cursing and crying, then she stop asking me questions and start asking them of God. "Why?"

She got back to me with, "That's it girl. *Estoy halta!* I'm calling your father. I'm sending you to Puerto Rico! It's about time he take up his responsibility."

That's nothing I ever heard my mami say. Bad as things could be, she ain't never wanna ask my father to take me, on account of she know that little as we got, Papi got even less on account of they ain't no good jobs in Puerto Rico. Mami say that people in Puerto Rico is so poor that half of them ain't even got shoes.

I beg my mother, "Please don't make me go there."

That's when she look at me and see my fear. She say that Papi had got the help he needed when he left us three years ago, and that he not messing with them drugs no more.

Like how she could know that for sure, if she ain't even know he was messing with them while he was living with us.

As she picked the phone lock on Ana's phone, I thought back to the day that my father told me that he had to move there to live with his mother. When he admitted to me that he needed help, because he was on drugs. And how I ain't never seen't my father since …

"Please Mami, no." I tasted the *Parkay* on my numb busted lip, wishing she had hit me with the broom instead.

I hate margarine, and I hate butter. I hate the taste, and I hate the smell. I even hate to look at it and anything that looks like it. I haven't eaten it since I was real little, when Papi used to spread it on his big Italian bread and toast it in our oven on Sunday mornings.

Even though I had to taste that *Parkay* with every word, I begged my mother not to send me to Puerto Rico. I tried to disconnect the call twice, as she dialed, but she held me back.

"I don't wanna go see him. You can't make me go!" I fall to the floor crying and begging.

When she hangs up, I stop long enough to think, and I think, my father must have heard me.

I don't care if he did. I don't care if I hurt him, and now I don't care if I hurt my mother neither, 'cause her mind is made up, and her foot is down. She sending me to Puerto Rico and I have to stay with my father for the rest of the summer, no matter how much I cry. I don't deserve the punishment.

My father went there when not even Brownsville could handle his bad, and now my mother is sending me there with him, to burn in the hot sun and live in the Puerto Rican mountains with a bunch of people that I can't hardly understand and that will never understand me.

I go to my room. I could still hear my mother talking to God in between the other phone calls she just has to make. She will spend the rest of the night from mad to sad on the phone, telling all my aunts and uncles what happened, saying I look like a monster, "*feisima*", and that every time she look at me, she 'on't know who she looking at. Finally she stops calling

67

after my aunt Big Luzzy loans her the credit card that would buy my airplane ticket to Puerto Rico.

In the three days that go by until I have to leave, I hardly leave my room. It is slow, like waiting for a ambulance after being shot. People all around me, just trying not to be near me. I could see them wanting to make that terrible t-t-t sound, that say "too damn bad."

My sister came in and out of our shared bedroom acting like I ain't even alive. She ain't even complain when I left my drawers opened, like she know that I am a lost cause, like she better than me, and soon she won't have to share her space with me. The worst is that she ain't even say nothing about her jacket.

Ana ain't never give Mami or nobody a day of trouble, and I look real bad bein' in the same space with somebody as good as her.

My room door is right across from the bathroom, so I slid in there when I absolutely can't hold it no more. Danny saw me, but he ain't say nothing to me. My brother Big Head Benjamin came in my room and said that I looked like I got jacked real bad.

He made sure that Ana was there when he said the word "jacked" too, so Ana could hear him and think about her once beautiful, favorite jacket. But I look worse than jacked, if you ask me. The black and blues along my neck and face are turning purple and green faster than I expected, but still not fast enough.

Mami musta been trying not to look at me neither, 'cause when I got back from my shower, she had put a old beige suitcase on my bed. I recognized it from my hater grandmother's closet.

I stuff all the summer clothes I have in that suitcase.

Then I go back to the bathroom and take Mami's yellow lipstick-looking concealer from the medicine cabinet. She only use it for whenever she got a pimple. She usually get them when she get her period, or when she eat chocolate. But since she sending me to Puerto Rico, I don't care. I wish she gets a whole bunch of pimples all over her face when I'm in Puerto

Rico, and everybody sees them. And when she looking real hard for her yellow stick I hope she realizes that I took it.

When Mami see the suitcase is ready she start crying like she ain't have nothing to do with it.

"Please don't make me go. I promise I'll never do nothing like that never again."

But Mami say, "No, Teddy is coming to get us" and she orders me to finish getting ready.

Teddy is my aunt Evelyn's latest boyfriend. He always out back of my *titi* Evelyn's apartment fixing his old black *Oldsmobile*. There is always something or other wrong with it. The back door on the passenger side is welded shut, but the other three doors work. My *titi* Evelyn loves that car 'cause the windows roll down by pressing a button. When he tinted them windows, she swore it could pass for a *limousine*.

Inside the car and on our way to the airport, it feels and looks like a hearse. Mami's crying, and I'm wearing black sunglasses to hide my face. I pray for the whole ride that the old car would break down, so I could miss my flight. Mami would lose her money and still have to find a way to pay my aunt Big Luzzy back. Serve her right.

I could see Teddy looking at how bad my face look from his rear view mirror, but he ain't saying nothing to me. When he first got with my aunt Evelyn, he always used to say that I was pretty like her, but he not saying it now.

This *Oldsmobile* is the only thing making a sound. I focus on the clouds that look like they following me all the way to *John F. Kennedy Airport*. These clouds make shapes, first I think that they are horses that I could ride on to escape, but they soon change into faces that laugh at me for ever thinking I could.

Curbside at the airport, I could see people saying their goodbyes. As Teddy pulls my stupid-looking suitcase from his trunk, I see a man kiss his wife goodbye in the car parked just ahead. There's also a real old black lady with a cane in one hand, a handkerchief in the other so she could catch her tears, is hugging a whole van full of people. A young perfect family of four, each blonder than the next, steps out of a real *limousine* looking like they out of a *Sears* catalog. They luggage has wheels, but is still taken on a cart by a airport worker, and the father slips him a five.

Everywhere I look is people not wanting other people to leave. Everywhere but in the black *Olds*.

My mother hugs me. The last thing I want to do is hug my mother, so I just let her hug me. Not knowing why I even do that.

Mami say, "This is for the best. I love you."

"The best for who?" I yell trying to embarrass her.

I could see the sorry in her face, but it wasn't enough to make her change her mind. She hands me to a plane guardian come to escort me—I am a underage minor—alone. Me and the lady walk and I could feel my mother watching me. I hope she thinking about how sorry she is. In a count of twenty I will turn around to look at my mother again. I will pull down my sunglasses and she will see me crying.

But she didn't.

She was already back in the car, crying into the dishrag she brought with her. I thought I saw Teddy wave goodbye, but then I realized he was just flicking his *Newport 100* out his window.

As he pulls away, his music come blasting out his radio. A *Run DMC* song feels like a real bad joke that only Big Head woulda been mean enough to plan.

This plane ride to Puerto Rico is not my first. First time I ever flew to Puerto Rico was when I was a newborn. It was so that my grandmother, Papi's mother, could meet me.

Second time was when I was nine. It was with my papi but this time also with my uncle Raul. Me and Papi had seats, but my uncle Raul was in a coffin underneath the plane, dead as he could be.

Raul was my father's brother. Raul had dark skin with slicked-back black hair. He was in a wheelchair long as I know him. I don't know why. It was a miracle he ever got anywhere, 'cause he always needed one free hand to hold his beer. I ain't never seen my uncle Raul without a brown bag over a *Budweiser*. His beer stink used to come out the pores on his face, smell't like my building's elevator on a late Saturday night.

Before Raul died, Papi was real careful how he used his credit card, but on the night he learned his brother died he took us all to eat at a Chinese restaurant where we could sit down. Mami got two *Tom Collins* drinks and was saying that Raul's liver ate him alive. Later, Papi put our plane tickets and the whole funeral on his *American Express* too. Like life was short and he knew that he never was gonna be able to pay it off anyway.

This time I am alone, wishing I was dead so Mami could be sorry and so I wouldn't never have to open my eyes and ever see my father again.

I sit between two fat ladies. Both stealing my armrests. One smell like my brother's sweaty basketball jersey whenever her creases part. The other one, like the three *alcapurrias* she has wrapped in aluminum foil. She eats them—one right after the other—as soon as we take off. It's like watching a *Nathan's* hot dog eating contest at Coney Island. I am still able to make out the highway below, as she takes her last mouthful. Her mouth swings open and I can see the meat grinding between the gaps in her teeth. The grease from the *alcapurrias* slides down her chin, and onto her red sweatshirt that say MERRY CHRISTMAS—even though it's summer.

It's a three hour plane ride to Puerto Rico. But I rather stay up in the air forever. As soon as that fasten seatbelt light turns off, I shoot up and walk to the back of the plane, with my little purse, inside of it a black comb, five dollars and my mother's concealer. I stay in the back by the bathrooms. The stewardess gives me a *People* magazine but it's *People en Español* and I hardly know any stars in it, and even though I could read in Spanish a little bit, I don't want to.

I want to vomit.

I watch people go in and out of the bathrooms. I wonder, as they stare at me, if they are trying to see my bruises, wondering what happened to me, or if they is just staring at *Charo* on the cover of my magazine. I want to talk to somebody, but everywhere I look is *jíbaro* faces.

A *jíbaro* is a dumb Puerto Rican. A total hick. Like a country bumpkin, 'cept with clothes that are too tight, high-water pants and nothing that matches. No manners. No sense. Too dumb to be mad or sad for too long. Too stupid, too ugly, too *jíbaro* —faces all looking forward to getting to where they are going.

When the plane is about to land, the stewardess says I gotta go back to my seat. Thank God, there is an empty seat behind my row. I make my way to it. A man gets there just after me.

"Excuse me, I think you're in my seat."

I didn't move. My expression pretends "I no speak no English." The stewardess hurries behind him and tells him that he has to take a seat now.

Any seat!

She makes him sit in the seat that had been mine.

He squeezes between the two ladies that are now sleeping. I didn't mean to play him like that, but it's only for a few more minutes.

"Bienvenido a San Juan, Puerto Rico."

I nearly jump out my skin, when a sudden and wild applause rings through the whole airplane. The two ladies in my former row awaken. They holler and hoot as their arms nudge the man at each of his sides but even he is too happy to feel bothered.

All that happy… I can't help but feel madder.

As I step off the plane, I could feel the warm air floating up through the ramp. It is long and hot, but the sweat marks on my shirt have nothing to do with the air around me. I wipe above my lip and the inside of my elbows and follow the crowd following the signs that say:

THIS WAY TO BAGGAGE

The sign should say: ELAINE, IN JUST A FEW MINUTES YOU GONNA SEE YOUR BROKE-DOWN FATHER.

Papi should be embarrassed to see me. How he could look me in the face without feeling the same shame he felt the last time I saw him? Before we ever knew that my father was on drugs, Mami always used to tell us that drugs are for weak people, and that if you got a strong mind, you won't get caught up in that mess. And even though Mami said my father was doing alright now, and got the help he needed, I haven't been able to erase the memory of the look on his drawn face, the last time I saw him.

The last time I saw him felt like the first time I ever really saw him. The real him, not the father that I loved, but like no father nobody could, should, or would ever love. Not the star baseball coach, or the conga-playing, salsa-singing rumba man that made everybody stop and stare. He was a strung-out, weak-minded loser.

The airport hallway never ends. I step into the ladies restroom and wet my face. I use the yellow cover-up stick again to try to hide my black eye. My face is still swollen from the beating, and the inside of my eye is still bloodshot but, with my glasses on, no one could notice. It's hardly noticeable—I hope. Maybe I am just getting used to seeing myself like this. Don't matter which is right.

Out of the bathroom and through the passage whose sign reads: NO RE-ENTRY. I step onto an escalator behind the lady who ate the *alcapurrias*. I hide behind her, not even wanting to peek out. *Jíbaro* island music plays on my way down. This is hell.

I am trying not to look down 'cause I don't want to see my father, ever. So I look up. There are big trees in front of me ... palm trees. The big windows all around the airport make a clear view of all the beautiful palm trees that sway like fans.

I look down. Family members wait at the foot of the escalator, but not one of them is for me. Not one of them is my papi. Some hold flowers and others little Puerto Rican flags like if they is color guards. Some is looking at me to see if I belong to them, making me feel worse. The people in front of me hug and cry and meet up with their family, but no Papi. If I could die from embarrassment, I surely wish I would right now.

I scan the whole baggage area before deciding to go back up again, not knowing why I would ever want to come back down again.

This time I will not look at them trees, no matter how hard they wave at me. He is not here. No Papi. No big deal ... except it is. I can't wait to tell my mother that I am at the airport alone. She will be so sorry for sending me here to some loser, too drugged out to remember to pick up his only kid.

I could see my suitcase riding away from me on the carousel, surrounded by all those happy people at the foot of the escalators, who were now impossibly even happier than before. I watch my bag as it comes around again—my grandmother's beige suitcase held together by a belt with pink and red ribbons, which Mami made sure to put on it so I could recognize it.

As I pick it up, I turn to see the palm trees again, and then ... I see my father. I could hear my breath vibrating in my head as my heart races inside. It's the kind of racing you feel in your heart when you about to get robbed.

He looks ... good. He has a healthy glow about him. Not the kind you get from sitting outside all baby-oiled down with a reflector, like my *titi* Evelyn do, or the kind the cops get from chasing after a criminal, neither. No, it's the kind you get from just being. Y'know?

Papi's old familiar swagger brings him to the foot of the escalator, the palm trees looking like his backup dancers now. I watch him get there, and I watch him wait. He looks disappointed, sad that I'm not there. Like he was hoping I was coming.

I want him to be that same mad I am—or was—but something else inside my heart make me reach out my arm and call out to him.

"Hey Papi! Papi!"

He looks over in my direction and I wave even harder. Papi could see me. And I could see him.

"Hey," I say, not being able to help the way my voice crack when it come out.

Papi stands glowing at me. His happy make the other happy that people all around him have, seem sad. He's the happiest person here ... maybe in the whole world.

My eyes go red underneath my sunglasses, and I hear my heart beat like I ran up twelve flights. I look up at the ceiling to try to stop my tears, but my pool empties in one blink. I squeeze my eyes tight to get it all out, like I was wishing real hard.

When I opened them, Papi is standing in front of me.

He hugs me ... the kind of hug that you give when you ain't seen somebody in three years.

And I am hugging him back ... the kind of hug that you give when you've been missing somebody for three years, or maybe for your whole life.

Walking to the parking lot, neither one of us ain't have anything to say. Everything just kinda feel weird. Like I don't know him no more and he don't know me. Even Papi's car ain't nothing like the *Chevy Laguna* he used to drive in Brownsville. His Puerto Rican car is a little blue hatchback and it have a big sign on its roof top that say *"FLORES"* ... which means Flowers in Spanish.

Papi opens the car door for me and I sit inside. I watch Papi from the side view mirror as he opens the hatchback and stuffs my suitcase between a bunch of red roses and a wreath of white flowers that say REST IN PEACE.

Turns out my papi is a flower delivery man now.

Papi drives, windows down. The keychain in the ignition holds my latest school picture inside a plastic frame. I look out at Puerto Rico so that I can avoid my father's eyes.

I could feel him looking over at me, but I ain't got nothin' to say, and Papi just drives.

I hold my head out and catch a glimpse of myself on the side view mirror. My sunglasses do a good job of hiding my bruised face.

Then Papi say, "You know you are wearing my sunglasses."

And I shrug, and Papi don't say nothing else.

We get off the highway drive through streets with buildings ... nothing like my *Langston Hughes* projects. These building is all white with orange tile roofs, and they got balconies and they are overlooking a beach and they look like a dream and heaven and a movie all in one.

Papi drives past a real pretty fountain and up to a gate. A security guard, wearing all white and looking like somebody out of *Fantasy Island*, comes out from his little gate house and ask

Papi where he going.

"*Flores para 3603.*"

The gate opens.

Papi pulls up to the main building and say that he gonna be right back. He gets the red roses from the trunk and disappears into the cloud of luxury.

I look behind me and catch the ocean sparkling a blue that I ain't never seen on ocean water at *Jones Beach*. A man walks beside his little girl, who strolls her baby doll carriage and I think that girl might be the luckiest girl in the world … to be living here and to have a doll carriage and to have a father that is walking beside her, slow enough that she could take her sweet time to get to where she going without nobody calling her slow poke.

Papi taps on the top of the car and grabs my attention. Papi hands me his key chain and says, "Switch seats. You're driving."

"I don't know how to drive." I say, and Papi say, "You will know after today."

I think I been dreamin' 'bout being able to drive for my whole life, but somehow I foun't myself feeling that my father ain't deserve to give me happiness. My forgiveness shouldn't come with a driving lesson, and somehow he ain't got the right. … But I don't have the heart to break his spirit like that, 'cause all I could see in him is love and goodness, and so I take the driver's side and I take what I can get, while I can get it.

I used to think that going in reverse meant that you had to move your foot a certain way. Like press on the heel part of your foot but it turn't out that you just had to put the car thingy on "R" which stands for reverse.

I caught the hang of driving in the back parking lot of that big luxury building and the first place that I ever drove to was the *Suarez Funeral Home*, where Papi delivered the REST IN PEACE wreath. The second place was a *limber de coco* (coconut icee) stand by a kite park, where me and Papi watched kites fly and ate our *limber de cocos* until a dark rain cloud made us do otherwise.

Papi took over the driving on account of the rain came hard and fast. I was glad that it focused Papi's eyes on the road as he swerved to avoid the massive puddles that soon became the still and flooded streets of my *abuelita* and Papi's house.

Now of all the differences that exist between Brownsville and Puerto Rico, the very biggest difference is in my two grandmothers. Mami's mama and Papi's mami could not be more different than one another…in the way they look, in the way they act and in the way they love me.

Stepping into my *abuelita's* house was like stepping into a yellow world. Everything was yellow. The yellow brick linoleum under the yellow velvet sofa against the yellow floral wall paper, which wrapped through to the yellow kitchen cabinets and even the yellow refrigerator and stove, where my *abuelita* stood hunched over and cooking.

My *abuelita* turn't around when Papi kissed her. Her coke-bottle glasses couldn't hide the tears that well't up in her eyes when she seen me standing there in her kitchen.

Her love and tenderness poured from her arthritic hands as she cradled my face for longer than it felt comfortable. She lifted my sunglasses and I did not feel my bruises and she did not see them. *Abuelita* hugged me in a way that reminded me of the love and trust that used to live in my father's embrace.

My cousins and aunts and uncle arrived almost immediately and lightened the heaviness in my grandma's heart. My cousin, Maria Isabel, was two years older than me and even prettier than my cousin Cynthia from Philadelphia. She took me by the hand and ran me out of the crowd and to the back room where she put on the radio and played English music … which was the last thing I thought I'd hear in Puerto Rico.

Maria Isabel couldn't speak a lick of English but somehow knew all of the words to my favorite songs, even rap music. She asked me what every word meant, and I loved having all the answers that she had seemed to be waiting a lifetime for.

Abuelita came in and stole me back into the kitchen where she served me special foods that my Brownsville family reserved only for holiday feasts.

In Brownsville, the lot of us Puerto Ricans would form an assembly line to labor over the steps needed to prepare the *pasteles* that here, in Puerto Rico, felt like they'd been whipped up without a thought.

And that kinda sums up Puerto Rico for me. Life is easy, and like suddenly there's nothing to complain about, nothing more anybody could wish for.

11 CHURCH

Oh yeah, and then there's church in Puerto Rico.

I don't own dresses and the only skirt I packed was the mini skirt that my sister wore in her junior high school play, and so I had to put it on, on account of girls ain't allowed to wear pants in the kinda church that my *abuelita* belongs to in Puerto Rico.

Maria Isabel warned me that the people at *La Iglesia de Salvación Pentecostal* are all between a little and a lotta crazy. I didn't believe her as she stomped and cried and pretended to catch the holy ghost to get me prepared for what I would soon enter. Before long I learn't that she wasn't joking about it.

Maria Isabel don't normally go to church but she came just to "protect me from their madness." My *Abuelita* doesn't quite like Maria Isabel but she was okay with Maria Isabel going on account of she say that Maria Isabel need some church in her.

Papi drove us and let us out while he went to park. Maria Isabel and I each held one of my grandmother's fragile arms and walked her inside. Soon as we got our grandmother to the first pew she was sucked into the center of the hellos and blessings delivered by her blue- and gray-haired friends. Maria Isabel sensed our chance for escape. She told *Abuelita* that we had to use the bathroom. Maria Isabel grabbed me by my hand and led us toward the bathroom, looked back at our *abuelita* to be sure she was still distracted, then swooped me out of a side exit door. A group of teenagers sat on the floor surrounding an older boy who strummed a guitar and sang like a soft kiss must feel.

Maria Isabel grabbed his beautiful mouth in her hands and whopped a kiss onto his lips. She took a cigarette and lighter out from her 32AAA bra and puffed away. Maria Isabel's brazen acts felt like a cool self-acceptance that I had never witnessed in a teenager.

The door to the church was burst open by the surprising strength of my *abuelita*. *Abuelita's* eyes threw daggers at Maria Isabel who quickly dropped her cigarette and stared back at her with equal disapproval.

Abuelita grabbed me by the hand, her anger aimed squarely at Maria Isabel whose mocking expression disappeared behind the door as it closed.

Abuelita led me to a pew where I'd be trapped by her and the elderly tribe of gray-haired women she seemed to head.

The preacher man held his hands up and his eyes closed. The congregants followed and I watched, doing all that I could to hold back the laughter as I recalled Maria Isabel's spot-on impersonation of them as she prepared me for what would come. The congregants shook and hurled their bibles up. They prayed with their eyes closed tight. Their prayers became more determined as they began shouting to God. Tears streamed down their faces as they begged for the spirit to enter them.

I couldn't hardly understand the words they was saying, but the preacher kept telling them that while they could be in church, in "God's location", they needed to enter "God's dimension."

There was one thing that Maria Isabel could not prepare me for … the familiar talent that I thought I had succeeded in forgetting. My father stood behind a piano and played as everyone watched him with the same admiration everyone had for him at the Brownsville rumbas. I struggled to understand the Spanish when Papi spoke to the church goers, but what he said was something that I would never forget. He looked over them and said, "Please may I beg your forgiveness …" and then he asked the congregation to allow him the opportunity to sing something in English, for me, his daughter that was visiting from New York.

The churchgoers "awed," and my father sang to me the words that only he and I would ever understand, and in that moment I believed that my father was healed. In that moment the trust that I swore to never give, somehow took over and let me love him again.

That night while we drove home, Papi asked me in English, so *Abuelita* and Maria Isabel wouldn't know what he said, "Do you have anything you want to ask me?"

And I did have so much that I wanted to ask him, but instead I asked him how he foun't the nerve to sing in front of so many people.

And Papi told me that if he ever looked at the people it would make him nervous, like waiting to see from their expressions what he should be feeling, rather than just feeling it and so his trick was to just stare at the back wall and sing out.

Next night I looked toward that back wall at the church as a Papi sang ... and there it was—the exit door and the Jesus Christ on a cross above it.

12 MIRA MAMI

In the three weeks I spent in Puerto Rico, I gained twenty pounds. My grandmother would feed me as a sign of her love and I would eat as an acceptance of it ... and because it was always the best thing that I had ever tasted.

Our family meal times were sacred. Between breakfast and lunch I would walk to my cousin Maria Isabel's house and watch her clean like kids shouldn't be allowed to. She moved sofas and beds to sweep and mop under them, and took intermittent breaks to smoke cigarettes and drive herself crazy talking about the boy that she liked that got another girl pregnant.

The more time I spent with Maria Isabel, the more I came to understand that she was a wild child.

One morning Maria Isabel stole her brother's car and sped us down the highway to that pregnant girl's house, where she sat outside smoking cigarettes and cursing saying how she wished "that pregnant bitch would show her ugly freckled face" so she could "bash it in!"

Although Maria Isabel was sixteen and older than me, I was taller than she was and, thanks to my grandmother, a lot fatter too. I prayed that I wasn't being seen as the brute force she brought to back her up in the pregnant girl's beat down ... In truth I had never picked a fight before. I always listened to Mami when she told me to avoid trouble and only fight if you can't run away.

The pregnant girl watched from her window and screamed out that she was going to call the police. Thankfully the threat was enough for Maria Isabel to drive us away and back to my grandmother's house in time for lunch.

Papi always joined us at lunch. Flowers could be stacked high in his hatchback, but he always took the lunch hour to fill his belly with my grandma's love, delicious food and both our company.

One afternoon our lunch was interrupted by a knock on the door.

No one knocks in Puerto Rico. We just enter as if we belong.

Papi went to answer the door and my curiosity made me follow. My mother stood in the doorway, more beautiful than I had ever seen her.

My father's mouth dropped as my mami said, "Aren't you gonna let me in?"

Papi opened the door wider and he hugged Mami in a way that was meant only for the big finales in romantic movies … that moment when two long lost lovers realize that they should have never been apart.

My grandmother's hostile words broke their moment and suddenly I realized that my two grandmothers had more in common than I thought. She said something like, "Look what the cat dragged in."

Papi broke the tension as he led me to hug my Mom. Last I'd seen my mother, I hated her for making me come to Puerto Rico. Now all of that was gone, and all I could think of was the possibility of life returning to the happy times that we had as a family, where even seeing a girl die was not the end of our happiness, but led to our deeper appreciation for life and what we had.

Papi lead my mother to the lunch table and my *abuelita* sat angry. Her soup spoon hit the plate hard with every dip. Her anger grew as she watched their sparks fly as my father called my mother beautiful.

At last, *Abuelita* slammed her plate and called my mother the devil.

All hell broke loose in Puerto Rico. *Abuelita* paced around my mami like she was a gang member about to punch her. Suddenly my little slow-moving grandmother was spry as a double dutcher.

Abuelita raced to the living room and back again, this time holding her green seven-day prayer candle. She held it up to my mother like she was about to put a hex on her ... or perform an exorcism.

Papi got in front of *Abuelita* like a shield to protect Mami. He stood at her and cried without saying a word. Then he grabbed me and my mother by the hand and led us out of the house. We loaded into Papi's hatchback. I sat squished between flowers as Papi drove in silence to a kiddie park.

Although I was too tall for those monkey bars and too fat for the swings, I still did as my father asked when he told me to go play in the park.

I squeezed into the swing and watched my parents' silhouettes as they became one.

Was I seeing things?

Were my parents kissing?

My smile was uncontrolled as I thought of the prospects of Mami and Papi being back together. I would feel safe again in Brownsville and we could have a car again ... and he could ...

And suddenly I thought of my papi singing in his rumbas and I looked deep into the memory and my knowledge of those project courtyards where the rumbas were held ... where I watched drug deals, and I thought of Papi being around that and I got scared.

Papi's horn honked ordering me to re-enter the car. Papi drove me and Mami to a hotel, where I stayed with Mami that night ... the night before we would return to Brownsville.

On that plane ride back home, Mami sat on the aisle and I sat at the window. Sitting sandwiched between us was a man, and that man was not my father. Mami turned to that center seat and asked, "Sir do you mind if we switch seats so I can sit beside my daughter?"

The man switched seats and Mami held my hand.

I looked out of the airplane window and said a silent goodbye to Puerto Rico and to my father.

13 DREAM LOUD

Back when I was in the 4th grade I remember having to do a diorama and a book report on WHAT I WANT TO BE WHEN I GROW UP.

I ain't had no idea what that was, and that was the first time I ever thought of it, apart from wishing that I could be a princess or a movie star, of course. My sister, Ana, who is four years older than me, she said that I would make a real good lawyer and so I drew a judge on a judge bench and a lawyer (me). We used a *Nabisco* cracker box on account of we ain't buy no new shoe boxes for a long time. I covered it with brown bag paper and on the top I wrote "I Want To Be A Lawyer" in big block red letters. Now that I am trying out for different high schools, I am forced to think about what I want to be again, in a more serious way.

See, there are all kinds of high schools in New York, and when you live in any of the five boroughs, you get to try out for whichever high school you want. Except for zoned high schools. You ain't gotta try out for those. Every neighborhood has a zoned high school. Them high schools is for people who want to stay close to home or for people who can't get in nowhere else. Our zoned school is *Wingate*—and believe me when I tell you that nobody, NOBODY, NOBODY wants to go *Wingate*. Cause nobody wants to stay in Brownsville, if they could help it. I mean you only go here if you got no choice, or if you got no plans of going to school at all. They got metal detectors at the main entrance, make it feel more like visiting day at *Riker's Island* prison than school. Not much learning going on there. Even the graffiti is spelled wrong.

My two brothers go to *Eli Whitney*, where they are learning to make furniture. Ben is real good at it. He started by making little jewelry boxes, and this year is his third year and he made a whole big TV cabinet where the TV slides out from behind closed doors and everything. His teacher even offered him a job just as soon as he graduates.

My sister went to *Brooklyn Tech*. Tech is one of only three science high schools. They are the hardest schools to get into in the whole city. I took the test for Tech because my reading and math scores is real good, and my teacher made me. But I don't wanna go there.

Going down the list of all the high schools in New York City feels like looking through the *TV Guide*. So much to choose from, wishing you could get to them all.

Like *Maxwell*, which is a school for cosmetology—which might sound like you studying planets and space ships but is really just doing peoples hair. Nereida's daughter Jenny went there. When I think about my future and all the things that I could be, I could definitely see me hanging around a beauty parlor making people look pretty. Every holiday, me and my Mom always put make up on my slow aunt Elizabeth and my even slower aunt Miriam. They go from zero to hero, and me and Mom are kind of like the mice in *Cinderella*. And even though the dress-up and make up don't last, they still look better than they do all the other days of the year ... and so *Maxwell* is definitely a good school for me to consider.

There is another good school I really would like too. It's called *Fashion Industries*. At *Fashion Industries High School* you learn how to design and make clothes. Being younger than my sister by four years makes all my clothes hand-me-downs and out of date ... by four years. You gotta get creative. Lately I been putting big safety pins on the bottom back of my jeans legs and tying shoelaces that connect them and make the jeans super tight around my ankle all the way up to my knee. This way wearing all my sister's old bell bottoms ain't like wearing her old bell bottoms at all. So the thought of sewing my own clothes and designing them feels right for me too. I could see myself doing that for sure.

Last week I took the test for *Fashion Industries*. It was a real easy reading and math test and then on the back page was a blank sheet, saying: Question #35: A rock band is coming to town. Use this page to draw an ad campaign for them.

I am a good drawer, always have been. On the bottom of each and every rap I write in my spiral notebooks I draw a picture. The picture is usually just of my eyes that express how each of my rap songs make me feel when I am done writing it. Ever since I was little, on my report card my teacher would comment, "Elaine is very creative. She should have a career in the arts."

I thought about going to a school like *Automotive* too, where you learn how to fix cars, 'cause I kinda like the idea of a girl knowing how to do things they not really supposed to know how to do. Like if a girl is named Jesse. Surprising! I like that. Last year when name belts first came out, I bought one with the name ANGEL. That's my father's real name and I just thought it was nice for a girl to call herself ANGEL. But ain't nobody called me that and so I gave it up.

Automotive school is mostly boys, so I would likely not have any problems getting a boy to like me. The odds would definitely be stacked in my favor. I bet if I called myself ANGEL there first off, everybody would call me Angel.

There is another school I would really like to go to. There is TV shows made about high schools like this, where they do singing and dancing and everything. The school is called the High School of the Performing Arts. They ain't got no test over there—not on paper, at least. There they got something called AUDITION. Pronounced AW-dition and thinking about it is AW-ful.

The thing is I gotta sing a song.

While I have been writing rap songs for many years, I am

no where near as good as *Roxanne*. *Roxanne* is a girl rapper that answered back to a guy rap who made a song about her called "*Roxanne, Roxanne*." Their rap about *Roxanne* was a real big hit, but her answer back to them was a even bigger hit.

Roxanne was the first female rapper I ever heard, and so ever since then, I been thinking that rapping might really be something that I could do.

I write all kinds of songs. I got a real good one about being a superhero, and getting rid of all the crime in Brownsville. I once had the courage to rap it for my uncle José and he said that it was real good. Almost like a gospel rap. 'Cause it was nice and wanting the best for people.

But mostly my raps are really more like poems. I got one about divorce and another about child abuse. The child abuse one sound so good that my 8th-grade English teacher called me into the principal's office with her to see if I was getting beatings at home.

She said that the lines was so good that it kinda had to be true. It went like this:

> Why does Mommy hit me with her belt and her shoe?
> I look to myself for the answer
> Reading between the black and blue

That was a real good poem. I am proud of that.

But I told my teacher, I write about feelings … not just mine, but what I see all around me. That particular poem was inspired by a TV show called *Good Times* when this lady's foster daughter, was getting burnt with a iron by her real mother. That episode was so good that it made me cry. I love that show. At the end of it, the girl chose to be with her foster mother, instead of her real moms.

The one I wrote about divorce said this:

> Separation of all assets, including a human life.
> All that is left of a man and his wife.

Rap songs are just poetry and I am good at it. My poems

are fill't with smart words that don't make no sense to use everyday. My beatboxing is getting better everyday too.

I think about the TV shows and movies like *Fame* and I think that the *High School of the Performing Arts* is where I belong, somewhere where I could just pop into song, and dance up a storm in the middle of the lunchroom. I ain't never do nothing like that, but it sure looks like fun on TV, and if I could just connect with a piano player and a dancer and some other kids like me, we could start a group and maybe be rich and famous one day.

My papi used to sing and play every instrument. You gotta think that, if the right person saw him, he woulda been bigger than *Tito Puente*. Sometimes I think that maybe I got that part of Papi somewhere inside of me.

I find myself praying on it again lately, asking God to make it appear. Just a little… anything.

Trying out for the *High School of the Performing Arts* is something I don't want to let anybody know that I am doing. It's embarrassing to have dreams of being a performer. Easy to make fun of. Easy to get crushed. Like the time that I ran down the stairs on my way to school, so excited to tell anybody my new rap song. I called Sandra Garcia on the lobby intercom. I couldn't wait to share it, but she stopped me and said, "I ain't got time to hear any of your childish rap songs. Grow up."

I stopped sharing after that. Stopped dreaming out loud.

Until now. Just trying out for the *High School of the Performing Arts* is dreaming out loud. Looking to my left and to my right and all I see is kids like me sitting quiet, yet still, they're dreaming out loud.

"Number 3769 we are ready for you"

And so there I stand, number 3769. You ever hear of that expression, teeth chattering and knees knocking? Well, it turns out that it ain't no expression after all. It is what actually happens when you that NERVOUS. I ain't never been this nervous in my whole life, not even when me and Mami got robbed in the elevator. Not even when I seen't a guy get shot.

Not even when I watched that *Mack* truck hit that little girl. Not even when that guy had tried to rape me, on account of them are things that you gotta react on without even thinking about. But this thing just got me thinking and thinking and waiting. Waiting long enough that the fear keeps creeping deeper and deeper inside me.

When they call't my number again, I put on the biggest smile that I knew how....but I could still feel my teeth clacking together. The shake was all over my body. Felt like I was covered in HEAT. Heat that made you shake from its cold and sweat from its hot. I prayed that I wouldn't pee my pants. As I walked up to the microphone in the middle of that room, I felt big eyes on me. Bored people waiting for me to un-bore them. Got me to thinking that maybe that nice shake in *Whitney Houston's* voice came from these here kinda nerves.

Here I go ...

A old lady said " Tell me your name, the name of the piece that you are doing and who wrote it."

"Hi. My name is Elaine Del Valle." I could hear the shake in my words. As I spoke, the microphone shrieked, and everyone in the room gave a look that I hoped would not be permanent.

"The name of the piece that I am doing is 'Out My Window What I See.'"

I took a deep breath, ready to begin—"Oh, and it's by me ... I wrote it."

Another deep breath, this time with my eyes closed, in and then out. I opened my eyes and I stared at the clock in the back of the room, the way that Papi had stared at the Jesus Christ at the back of the church. And I rapped, like the real *Roxanne, Run-DMC, Jay Z* and *Will Smith.*

> I see attacks
> It's wack
> The crime is black on black
> Some crazy dirty ho just sold her baby for some crack
> I see the haters, the players

The bosses never pay us
The dirty old men that say
They want to date us

I puckered for my beat box and let it out. It sounded real good on the mic and I was 'bout to start dancing like a scene out of *Fame*–

"Excuse me—Excuse Me!"

The old lady stopped my magic and asked, "Can we hear a song?"

I stood there confused and sweating worse than before. My upper lip was wet with salty sweat.

"A song that you could sing? We asked that you prepare a song. Did you prepare a song?"

And right there, I knew it wasn't gonna happen for me. 'Cause to me, that was the song that I could sing. That was the song that I had prepared. I thought "NO! I don't know a song, lady, 'cause that is my song," but my mouth said "Yeah, yeah, sure I know a song"

And at that moment, my mind went blank. I could think of *Whitney Houston* and *Mariah Carey* but I couldn't think of one song. Not one word in any of their songs. The only song that I could think to sing was the national anthem—and not the one "Oh, say can you see." 'Cause of my father and all his baseball games, yo I can't stand that song. I could only think to sing the song that I have had to sing five days a week since I was in Kindergarten. It's the black national anthem.

And so I stepped back up to the microphone and stared at that the back wall again—picturing Papi's church exit sign and the Jesus Christ that hung above it.

"This here … is the black national anthem."

Oh my God. Who wrote it? Who wrote it?

I have no idea who wrote it, but let's face it, the chances of these people knowing this song, I may as well say "*Cool Mo Dee*" and the *Real Roxanne* wrote it, but instead I chose to say, "It's by Mimi Marshall and Sandra Garcia".

After all, they not gonna know. And then I began

Lift every voice and sing
Until earth and heaven ring
Ring with the harmonies
Of liberty
Let our rejoicings ri—

And that's when the old lady said, "THANK YOU."

I said, "You're welcome," but inside I kept thinking "They ain't have to cut me off right at the good part."

All the way home I sat on that Double L train thinking, if I was in the *Fame* school I might get up and sing what just happened, while jumping from train car to train car. Dancing to the rhythm of the double L train. Maybe I write the song and call it "Let Me In." Maybe the words should include "I gotta get out from where I am…I just got to."

But instead I sat tight in my seat between a mama and her boy playing with his *Spider-Man* and a man that smelled like the end of a six-day work week on double shifts.

I could still taste the nervous sweat on my upper lip, and I wondered if I would ever find a place where I felt I belonged.

14 WORK IT MAMI

Back in Brownsville seem't like so much has changed. Not in Brownsville, but in my family. Especially Mami.

Turn't out that Mami, while I was in
puerto Rico, had got herself a job.

She been working for the lawyers office on Stone Avenue called *Ornstein & Ornstein*.

My mami ain't never worked and she ain't never even got her high school diploma but suddenly she wearing make up and skirts and putting on high heels and going off to a real office to work, five days a week.

Turn't out that while I was in Puerto Rico, the twelve-year-old Latina girl from apartment 8B had got raped in our building. She was just walking down the stairs and got dragged up to the roof by some man, our building's roof that shoulda been locked. The girl's mama ain't speak no English and so she asked Mami to come with her to that lawyer's office to see if she got a case against the building. The lawyers took the case and a liking to my mami, said she was real professional like and that they could use somebody like her to translate for all their Spanish-speaking clients.

Mami took the job and they put a big sign up in the front that said "*Hablamos Espanol*".

Mami said she cried when she got her first paycheck and used it to come to Puerto Rico to get me. She thanked God for putting her in the right place at the right time.

My mami had been translating for my *abuela* at the welfare offices for as long as I could remember ... not never realizing that her Spanish was a skill that lotsa people needed.

Even though I always loved my mami and knew that she was always trying to do the right thing for everybody around her, I ain't never really think she had any kind of future outside of taking care of her family. I suddenly felt a new respect for my mami and in a way that made me sorta kinda got a new respect for myself.

I can't explain it.

My *abuela* been calling me a loser and my father a junkie for most my life and I been feeling like I could never say nothing to her ... feeling like she right and all. But now I kinda feel like I ain't gotta believe that no more.

We ain't bring Papi home, but home was never gonna be the same again. Mami was never gonna be the same again and I ain't never gonna be the same again.

Seem't like every one of Mami's paychecks brought new things into our lives. New clothes, new dishes, new bed sheets, new furniture, and even though Mami had always kept the cleanest apartment in Brownsville, it was now also the nicest and I was so proud of Mami. So proud of us.

Ana, who was the oldest of all of my *abuela's* grandkids was also the first one to go to college ... and now Ana was in love too. Even Benjamin seem't like he ain't deserve the "Big Head" name I used to call him. I 'on't know if it was Papi's Pentecostal church that did it but finally I felt myself believing in God.

15 HIGH SCHOOL

High school ain't fun like I thought it would be. *Brooklyn Tech* High School absolutely sucks.

The school is ten floors high and divided by east, west, south and north. I know that north is up and south is down, on account of I have heard lots a people from my block say they going "down south" which usually means they going to visit family in the Carolinas or "up north", which mean they going to jail, but north and south ain't up and down here, and so I ain't got no idea where I am or where I am going at any time and I am too embarrassed to ask, because if I do I will seem like the stupidest person in the whole building.

The locker, that I always dreamt of having since I seen the movie *Grease*, is way down in the basement where it smells and I can't open it anyways cause them round combination locks is the pits! And nothing like what you see on TV.

The boy that I wish liked me likes a girl from a place called Yugoslavia instead. I stare at him while he stare at her, and she —Anna Milat-Meyer—couldn't care less about either one of us on account of her blue notebook got pictures *scotch-taped* to it with her and her boyfriend. And all around them pictures is stickers of hearts and LOVE traced around them in black marker. Anna's boyfriend is black, which surprised me cause it always seem like white people like to stay away from blacks and Latinos ... but then again I ain't never really had too much to do with white girls my age, unless you count my cousins Nellie and Melody who is half Jewish.

My teachers don't care if I am here or not, and neither do anyone else. You could really disappear in a place like this ... and so I do.

Disappear.

Best thing about going to high school is going on a train to get here. The thing about trains is that every time you step into one you could enter another world. A world that gets far, far away from where you started as soon as the doors reopen, letting in new people that ain't got no idea where you started from or where you going.

On my Brownsville train platform I am still just a girl from the poorest, most criminal-minded district in New York. I step into that train as me, but when those train doors re-open and the new passengers step in, I could have come from just about anywhere--even the nicest neighborhood. I could be a spy on a secret mission.

Down the stairs and through the tunnel at Broadway Junction is where all kinda trains meet, even ones that don't got graffiti all over them and so, in a fish tank full of fish that I 'on't recognize, I am not recognized right back and so am anyone I want to be.

Everybody's clothes is different, like ain't no two people going to the same place. Each one got a personal fiesta going in they ears. Some bopping to they walkman music, others just looking out and not seeing nothing in front of 'em. Some is buried in thick books that they is almost finished with and others reading newspapers that they never will finish. Big newspapers and little ones. Black and white ones and some with color. All these people ... they all just acting like they want to be in their own world, a world that I prolly could only imagine. A world that I really want to get to know.

It is the third week of school now and my English teacher is a nasty short little lady with a heavy German accent. She sure don't know none of our names, not that she care to, and I still don't know my east from my west.

A boy that stopped to help me get to my second class on the first day seem to always be at that same spot where we met, at the same time. His name is Joey and he is kinda cute, except when he smile...His crooked teeth is too big for his mouth. And even though I think he like me, I can't help but wonder, if Anna Milat-Meyer passed by us, would he stop looking at me to look at her.

On the first day he walked me to my second class, and he ain't even seem to mind when the late bell rang. He told me more about himself in one trip from 1001 North to 231 East than I know about my next-door neighbor in all my 14 years.

Joey is a senior, and he is from Ecuador and so he likes soccer and he thinks that I am crazy for never having seen't a soccer game. He said that all Latinos know soccer, it's practically OUR sport, but I thought that was baseball. He make me feel like I am from another planet ... and I think I am ... a planet called Brownsville.

Joey is on the gymnastics team. He is short. He would even be shorter than me if he was to cut his hair. I really felt good that I knew what gymnastics was. "I like gymnastics," I told him. "I seen't gymnastics all this summer on the *Olympics*." I helped my aunt Evelyn all summer wit' her new baby daughter Kristina, and so I got to watch the *Olympics* from her hot cable box, which make any of the TV channels come in for free and real clear without even a antenna.

The gymnastics team meets next to the locker that I never go to on account of that stupid lock. I told him that I would go watch him do gymnastics today, and the bleachers was empty when I got here, but soon nuff a girl came sat right beside me, and she got yellower hair than I ever seen anybody have.

I seen't Joey and his team come out of the locker room.

"Who you here for?" she say.

"Joey," I say.

"He good" she say. "I am Dana."

And I say, "I'm Elaine. I'm a freshman. You got nice hair... the blondest hair I ever did see."

And she laughs and say that she what you call a "platinum blonde."

"Only thing I ever heard was platinum was a record album."

And Dana laughs again and say, "You funny, Elaine."

Dana got green eyes and freckles but she not pretty like you'd think those things would automatically make her. Her eyes and nose and mouth is all too close together for that, and I wonder who she there to watch, and so I ask.

"Who you here for?"

And she point to a boy that I think ... I know ... is definitely the best looking boy I ever seen in my life. He so good looking that he pretty, he at least a whole head taller than Joey next to him, and he look strong. And I am quick to look back at Dana on account of I just spent way too much time on a boy that somebody else, Dana, is here for. Then Dana say the best thing I ever heard in my life, "That's my brother, Brian."

Brian. Her BROTHER, Brian!

My eyes lay set on Brian so much that they teared up when something made me blink ... and that something was Joey calling out, "Hey Elaine."

"Hey," I say back, wishing that Brian would look my way, but he didn't.

No matter, 'cause I want the first time that Brian look at me to be special. I want him to look at me in the same way that the boy in my English class stare at Anna Milat-Meyer from Yugoslavia. Like he looking at a whole other country and his eyes just can't get enough.

Brian and Joey is practicing right next to each other and so I could stare at Brian all practice long without looking like a weirdo.

Them uniforms they wear for gymnastics look even funnier in person than on TV. They so tight that even though you not looking you gotta be extra careful to watch that you keep your eyes in the right place so not to feel embarrassed. Not that I want to look at no boy's private parts or nothing. Not at all, but can't hardly help but notice in them tight clothes how boys is so much different than girls is. Yuck.

Round Brownsville, won't no guy never wear nothing like that. Mostly they be walking around with they pants dragging and they underwear showing. Look stupid, but gymnastics suits don't look no smarter.

Dana keep talking to me no matter how little I say back and she just think everything I say, even "uh-huh," sounds funny.

"Where you live?" she asks.

And I say, "Brooklyn," and she say, "Me too."

Dana points up the block and say that she "live across the street in a brownstone."

"My building is made of brown bricks," I say and she laughed again.

"You should come over one day after practice and I can make you some pasta or something," and I say, "I will," but I am thinking I ain't got no idea what pasta is.

And so I say, "I 'on't like that," and she say, "You don't like pasta—not even spaghetti and meatballs?" and I say, "Oh you said pasta … I thought you said lobsta," and Dana just laughed again, and this time I laughed with her.

If only she knew.

Dana said, "I'll be right back," and I stayed to watch Joey and Brian as they practiced, taking turns on the bars. They was more muscle bound than any boys I ever seen't they age. Big muscles on they arms with real little legs. Seem like all them gymnastics people is built the same way. Me, I opposite that. I got a small top and bigger longer legs, makes doing something like a push up damn near impossible, even though I am much bigger and stronger than girls I seen in gym class that can do a hundred push ups.

Brian is built in a way that he could definitely do push ups. He is hauling himself up and flinging around his legs around them gymnastics bars like they is not even a part of his body.

And I watch and I watch, for the whole practice. Then it is over and Brian is walking in a whole 'nother direction from me. North, south, east, west … I ain't got no idea in which direction but it ain't at me.

I watched Brian get smaller as Joey walked towards me.

"Practice was good." I say to Joey.

"Thanks," he say back.

Then I could see platinum blonde Dana waving at me and hear her screaming from the other side of the gymnasium, "Hey Elaine, wanna come have some pasta at my house?"

And Brian start waving over to Joey, and he say, "Come on, guys."

I was just about to say yes but Joey scream't out, "We can't," and I ... I wanted to damn near kill Joey. I say "Tomorrow. Tomorrow. I'll come over tomorrow."

And Dana say, "Ok, tomorrow!"

Joey walked me to the A train station, and all the while I wished that he would fall into a manhole for not going to Dana and Brian's house...but I ain't say nothing instead I just listened as he told me that he live in the Bronx.

"Elaine, you know everything about me, and I only know that you have a terrible sense of direction." And with that Joey laughed at his own words. But I ain't laugh back. "Where you live?" he said, and I said, "I live on the other side of Brooklyn, like on the way to Canarsie," and he said, "What train stop?"

I ain't want to answer but then I figured that Joey ain't prolly know nothing about Brooklyn, in the same way I ain't know nothing about the Bronx, and so I said the truth. "Sutter Avenue, on the Double L."

"It must take you a long time to get to school then."

And I thought, depends on what he consider a long time. "About a hour. See you tomorrow."

"I'll walk you to your 2nd period."

"OK, I will be there and at gymnastics practice too, and we will have pasta with Dana and Brian. OK?"

After I said that, Joey smiled, trying not to show his big crooked teeth, and then he leant in and kissed me on the cheek.

Down them stairs to the A train, and all I could feel is weirded out by Joey's kiss on my cheek...Like it has left a permanent stain on my face for all to see.

When I got home I looked up the word "pasta" in the dictionary, and it say food made from flour. My mom don't even got flour in the cabinets. She don't cook nothing with flour. Our spaghetti come in a box. Then I look up spaghetti and it say "cooked string-shaped pasta," and it made my mouth water thinking about sitting across from Brian eating his pasta.

Next day, I sneak my sister's nice pink striped jeans in my book bag and change in the hallway, whole time thinking that these is the pants that I want Brian to first notice me in. They are perfect and better than everything I own put together. My sister Ana would kill me if she knew I was stretching them out.

It is perfect weather, and it take me the usual 15 minutes to walk to the Double L train. I climb the stairs to the platform one step at a time instead of my usual two on account of these pants is tight, and think I better not eat anything until pasta later, or these pants will surely rip—"Hi!"

At the top of them stairs on that platform of Sutter Avenue on the Double L was none other than Joey. His little gymnastics legs come all the way from the Bronx to Brooklyn —to Brownsville no less.

And I feel crazy ... crazy bad ... crazy guilty for thinking 'bout nothing but Brian. Crazy and kinda liking that Joey done come all the way out here to Brownsville. Some might say that he risked his life for me. Whenever my aunts moved to Queens or anywhere outside of Brownsville, they don't never wanna come back. They always inviting us to visit them instead. They say, "I ain't risking my life." Not even to visit their own mother. And so I think Joey is crazy. Crazy brave and crazy 'bout me.

And here we are standing crazy crazy ... standing still, I feel rattling crazy. All this rattling without a word.

"Hey," I say.

I stood on that top step not wanting to make a move. Joey was on the platform above me, taller than me for the first time, wearing a military jacket, trying to look tough. His lips working hard to cover his teeth. His *DA* haircut held perfectly by hairspray. Acting like being there, like what he done by being there, was no big deal. But it was. It was to me and it sure nuff would be to my aunts.

"Excuse me," said a lady behind me struggling up the steps with a cart behind her.

I stepped up to the platform and the Double L train came

roaring by us making his and my hair sway in its wind. When the doors opened Joey got in, holding the doors for me and said, "You coming?"

I walked onto the train and Joey spotted the one seat left. He ran to it and let me sit down while he strap-hung above me, taller than ever before.

After first period he was there. Joey. Waiting to bring me to my second period that by now I knew full well how to get to. Joey took my books as Anna Milat-Meyer walked by slower than she needed to and flinging her hair in his direction. But Joey flicked it away like you would a fly on a hamburger. And then he said to me, "Them are new pants, right? They look nice."

"Yeah," I said, "but they too tight. I don't think we should go for pasta after your practice. My zipper might split."

16 SILVER LINING

"Hey, Papi. Whass going on?"

Papi don't call too often, so when he do, I always 'xpect him to say that my *abuelita*—his mother—is dead.

Not that she sick or nothing, but my *abuelita* is the oldest person I ever seen. Her skin is so shriveled that it look like she been in a bathtub for a week, all the way in, except for her nose. And that's the kinda thing people gotta spend the money on a long distance phone call to tell you. Everything else could wait for the mailman.

"Is *Abuelita* okay?"

"Yeah. Yeah," he say. Funny when Papi say words like yeah, it almost sound like it's coming from somebody without a thick accent.

"I just want to talk. Do you remember the story of the 13?"

How could I forget? When I was real little, me and Papi had got into a elevator in a real big building in Manhattan, and I was counting all the buttons until I realized that they didn't have a button for the thirteenth floor. I asked this man whose job it is to work the elevator, "where is the thirteen?" and he say, "Thirteen is bad luck," and then I started to cry.

I couldn't get over the thought that I must be bad luck, on account of I was born on the thirteenth of July. Seven pounds and thirteen ounces. Twenty-six inches long—which is two times thirteen. Seem like ever since that time, I been hearing people reminding me, over and over and over again—especially when I turned thirteen on Friday the thirteenth—that thirteen is bad. And that superstition don't just hold true for Puerto Ricans! That there is something the whole world think alike on, like french fries, ice cream and blue eyes.

Papi tells me on the phone, in the same way he did when I was crying in that elevator, "Ever since you was born on the thirteenth, even those Friday the thirteenths have been nothing but great days for me. *Cómo* ... all of the bad tha's supposed to happen on that day couldn't hurt me, because it's the day you was born. When somebody tell me that it is a bad day, I look at them and I know, *yo sé*, that it could never be a bad day, not for me. Like they say *en Inglés*, 'the silver lining.' Every cloud has a silver lining. Elaine, you are my silver lining."

I know it's a parent's job to be making they kids feel special and all, but my father been saying nice things to me and most everybody that he see his whole life.

I used to think whatever he say sounds like words plucked right out of a song. Every song could be a poem that could put a smile on your face or make you cry, and sometimes... it could do both at the same time.

Like every day he spend a little time trying to figure out a new way to tell me he love me... and then he say...

"Elaine, I am dying."

A half smile comes to my face. The kind that makes you make a sound out your nose, while you waiting for the end of a joke.

But Papi ain't say nothing—for a while, like he letting it sink in and waiting for the smile to leave my face. And then—just like if he could see me—when it did, he said it again.

"I am dying."

And I say, "What?"

And I feel What? and nothing else.

"I have AIDS," Papi said.

And I—

drop.

Even though I haven't moved and I am still lying on my

mami's bed. The top of me feels like it's empty. Mami walks in front of me and I look at her and I know that she knows.

Much as I don't know what to say is as many things that is going through my head. And everything that dropped down on me is coming fast forward at full force—like vomiting from food poisoning. Bad stuff first—up, over and all around me.

I know about AIDS. I seen it.

All over Brownsville. People die quick.

They get skinny and they teeth rot out, and they get scars on they skin. It's like suddenly they look sick … sicker than being on crack, or even heroin.

They like the walking dead. Then they are dead.

On the news they show a whole bunch of gay people fighting for they rights. They show little kids got bad blood transfusions, and people feel sorry for them … 'cause they is good people. The other way to get AIDS is by being junk. They call 'em "junkies." Like *Abuela* (Mami's mom) used to call Papi. Them is the people don't nobody feel sorry for.

Across the street, there is a Puerto Rican family whose father died of AIDS last year. His daughter Vivian used to go to school with my brother Benjamin. After he died, everybody was talking about it. Make me feel real bad for that whole family.

Vivian's father was a heroin addict—like mine. Like mine was, 'cept hers never stopped being one.

The news be talking about junkies. "Heroin addicts spread AIDS by sharing dirty needles." Then they show a whole bunch of dirty needles peeking up from the sand on beaches—make you never want to feel the sand between your toes.

AIDS been getting so bad round here, the methadone clinics is giving away free needles to drug addicts, so that they don't gotta share.

Vivian's father used to hang out at the rumbas. And just like that all I could think is, Papi and him musta been sharing dirty needles.

I want it to stop, but my skin starts to crawl at the movies playing in my head of them together, listening to music and doing drugs. And I can't tell if they movies I am making up or memories I forgot I had. I think about open track marks becoming snakes eating me alive. I look down at the inside of my elbow and see my big purple vein underneath my skin, and I wish I could pull it out. But I swallow my thoughts and hope that Papi doesn't know what I am thinking.

The thing is, there ain't much to say when you know someone you love got the AIDS. Ain't gonna make no difference what you think, what you do, or what you say anyway.

Absolutely no difference.

"Can I call you back?" I say.

And before he could answer me, my phone is half way down.

I not crying. I not nothing. Mami's hand touches my shoulder as I get off the bed.

I walk to the bathroom and lock the door. I turn the water knobs as far as they could go, until they leak. I watch the hard, fast, loud water flow out our rusty spout and into our tub.

Taking off my clothes, I can't hardly recognize my red, wet, wrinkled eyes in our vanity mirror. And I hold my mouth to muffle the sounds I know need to come out of me. I cover my mouth, but I can still hear myself ... inside myself.

Long cries that don't let me take a break for air, and make me feel like they trying to kill me.

I lay in the tub, still holding my mouth. Gasping for air through my stuffed nose. The tub is filling too fast. I take the plunger out of the hole so I don't gotta turn off the water.

Above me are the dark clothes that Mami hung after washing last night. They dry, but I forgot to take them down like Mami told me to. I shoulda taken them down. They hanging over me and it feel darker than it gotta be.

I move my hand from my mouth, and I whisper: Drugs will put you in a box—coffin or jail—pusher or user—drugs will put you in a box.

Ever talk to yourself and think that maybe you crazy for doing it? Well, Mami say that that don't make you crazy at all, on account of God is everywhere and so you never really talking to yourself after all. You just really talking to God.

I talk to God and say:

"Let GO! LET GO! LET GO! LET GO!"

And then I let go.

For a long while.

I put the plunger back in and shut the water and stare at them clothes wishing I folded them last night.

I am there for so long and I notice for the first time, that my brothers or sister is not rushing me out of the bathroom. I don't have to shut the shower curtain while someone pees on the other side of it...or listen to Ana complain about her pimples while trying to make steam to help them be ready for popping. And that makes me think that they must know, and that they is leaving me alone on account of ... they love me.

And so I get out because I love them, and I fold my brothers' shirts and my sister's jeans, more carefully then I have ever folded them before. Careful not to leave more creases then there have to be.

I leave the bathroom and when I get to my room I see that my sister has removed the lock from her phone.

I dial Papi's phone number with my shriveled fingers. I sit on what used to be his side of the bed in Mami's room. I don't know what to say, but I know that I need to call him back.

In between rings, I could hear Mami's metal spoon stirring against her iron pot and I could smell her white rice. My favorite. White rice and not red.

After the third ring, Papi answers and this is what he said.

"*No sea triste, mija.* You can't be sad. Please don't be sad. I am not sad. I feel happy. Happy, because I have lived a good life—*una vida maravillosa, sí.* People that love me, baseball ... *mi musica.*"

I think about my two brothers, who still love baseball.

"Danny plays baseball in college now. Part baseball scholarship," I say as I realize it, trying to give more meaning to what he is saying.

But Papi doesn't need any more meaning to it. It's already his life's work, what made the life of a poor man so rich. And then I could hear the smile on his face when he says:

"See how proud I can feel. And *mi mama* is proud of me

and better than all of that, *mejor que todo*, I had you. Everyday I see jour picture on my keychain, and I know you have so much potential inside. You know that if there is another side, I will be with you, closer, much more closer than righ' now."

And suddenly, I believe it. Not because I want to believe, but because ... I truly believe. Like I could feel the wonder of it! I been looking out my window all of my life and feeling the wonder of the birds. Not the kind of birds that people like— fancy ones with different colors, or the ones that could repeat your words—the wonder of just plain old pigeons, the ones that be in Brownsville.

They say when birds fly in flocks that it means somebody just died. I'm not sure if everybody believes that, but it's what I believe, and believing that makes me sure that there is a God. Not in the way that Nereida Martinez's mother say she talk to the dead or that God talks to her, but in the same way that smiling at someone can make them smile back—in that way. Like being near a pillow and being able to smell the sleep in it helps me to sleep—in that way. Like hearing a good song and feeling the happiness of it—inside of me and all around me— in that way.

Me and Papi stayed on the phone all night, and Ana never came in to complain. I didn't know that it would be the last time I talked to my father.

Something new that I learn't about AIDS—is that it takes your mind away too. Makes you not remember the people you been looking at your whole life.

I took twenty-three baths in twenty-three days until the day my father died. I folded the laundry before each one.

I couldn't go to my papi's funeral. Even if we could have afforded the airfare, I didn't want to think of my papi like I thought of other people in the last stages of AIDS. I wanted to remember him like the time I last saw him. I wanted to remember my trip to Puerto Rico. In his church, he was happy singing ... everyone looking at him with respect and admiring him. Some of them never knew his past and some of them knew all of it.

I wanted to think of him in home runs and every conga

beat. In the parts of songs that make the hair on my skin rise.

He was thirty-six years old. I guess he always will be. Not sure if it is only me, but my father dying at thirty-six, makes me feel like I'm gonna go before I'm thirty-six. Like I gotta fold the laundry and get things done when I can, so I ain't gotta live under the darkness of not having done it.

Feeling like that might sound bad but actually it feels really good. It makes every thing feel important. Like it counts.

When I think of my father, I think:

People might never know who my father really was. They might think of him as a man who died at thirty-six on account of he got AIDS, on account of he was a drug addict and that is all that they will think.

But if my papi taught me one thing it is;
Don't matter what other people think.
And that I should see the silver lining.
I could be the silver lining.
Be the silver lining.

17 US

The year that Papi died (1989) was also the year that I graduated high school and that my family moved out of Brownsville.

My mother worked for the law firm for many years until she retired. She remarried and had a fifth child, which made me a big sister for the first time at the age of seventeen.

My older sister Ana married her childhood sweetheart. They have been happily married for over thirty years. Ana and her husband have seven children, including our family's first college graduate. Another of Ana's daughters is in college studying pre-med.

My brother Danny has three children and while his younger two children are still in college, his oldest is a college graduate on his way to being an actuary. Danny had a twenty-five year long career for a *Fortune 100* company. Upon his retirement Danny went on to start his own business and in 2019 was awarded his New Jersey county's "Best New Business."

My brother Benjamin became a master carpenter and to date works on remodeling homes.

As for me, I began my career as an actress. I studied acting at *Wynn Handman* studios in New York City's legendary *Carnegie Hall.* It was there I began to understand the shape of scenes and after two years with little Latinx-based stage plays to work from, I began writing what would become *Brownsville Bred* (a one-woman stage play). The writing poured out of me and I found myself waking in the middle of the night with childhood memories of the milestones that shaped me.

Within one year, my stage play, "*Brownsville Bred*" had won multiple festivals and was touring at high schools and colleges. *Brownsville Bred* became the most successful play in the 34 year history of New York City's legendary *Nuyorican Poet's Cafe* (where I self-produced). It was there that I was discovered by *Pamela Moller Kareman* who would serve as my director and finally bring *Brownsville Bred* to its official Off Broadway debut. The *New York Times* and other newspapers I watched my father read (like the *Daily News* and *New York Post*) raved about *Brownsville Bred*.

Brownsville Bred was my way of sharing my history while creating my father's legacy.

Brownsville Bred was soon recognized by a senior executive at the *HBO* network. She fueled my mission to continue writing and creating content that represented female and urban voices.

In 2019 my second short narrative film as a writer, director and producer made its network premiere on *HBO*.

My family didn't have many material possessions, but we had each other and a deep appreciation for life and the American dream that I deeply believe is available to all who choose to follow or blaze a path of continued perseverance and work toward goals.

I am a business owner, a film director, happily married, mother to a college graduate and now an author.

Dream out loud. Dreams come true.

ABOUT THE AUTHOR

Elaine Del Valle is an award-winning filmmaker. She began her career in storytelling as an actress. Her early successes were in the on-camera commercial and animation voice-over worlds. It was while studying professional acting at *Carnegie Hall*, under the legendary acting teacher, *Wynn Handman*, that Elaine began writing what would become her critically acclaimed, autobiographical stage play, *Brownsville Bred*. The stage play brought her to multiple wins on the stage festival circuit before she began to self-produce at New York City's legendary *Nuyorican Poets Cafe*. *Brownsville Bred* became the most successful play in the venue's 34 year history. Director, (and Artistic Director at the *Schoolhouse Theater*) *Pamela Moller-Kareman* attended Elaine's performance. *Ms. Kareman* became Elaine's director and would soon lead her on a journey that would include Elaine's (*Brownsville Bred*) first official off-Broadway run. *The New York Times* called the play "From Girlhood Trials to Onstage Triumph."

Elaine performed *Brownsville Bred* at schools (middle school through college) and for corporate events that would include *The Multicultural Media Forum* where *HBO's Lucinda Martinez* would discover Elaine's voice and inspire her to continue on the path of content creation. Elaine went on to create and write her first web series, *Reasons Y I'm Single* (alongside long time friend and colleague *Holie Barker*), which Elaine also produced and directed.

Elaine continued producing and shared her tools to support the work of other diverse talents struggling to make their voices heard. With her second web series, alongside Director *William D. Caballero*, Elaine became the first person to ever license an interstitial series to the *HBO* network (*Gran'pa Knows Best*).

As a director, Elaine has garnered several awards on the festival circuit, including for Best Director and Best Film. Her short film, *ME 3.769* was supported by a grant from the *Sundance Institute* and went on to make its network premiere on the *HBO* (2019).

Elaine was named *"Madrina"* (Godmother) at the *Prime Latino Media Salon*, *"Emerging Artist"* at the *Multicultural Media Forum* and in 2019 she received the Vanguard award from *Official Latino*. In 2019 *Miami New Times* named Elaine amongst their "Five Filmmakers to Watch." Elaine was featured as an inspirational figure in *Beating The Odds* (a *PBS* documentary) alongside such luminaries as *Michelle Obama*.

Follow Elaine on Instagram @elainedelvalleproductions

For more information on Brownsville Bred visit www.BrownsvilleBred.com

Made in the USA
Columbia, SC
26 January 2020